rockschool®

Drums

US Level 7 (UK Grade 7)

Performance pieces, technical exercises and in-depth guidance for Rockschool assessments

All accompanying and supporting audio can be downloaded from: *www.rslawards.com/downloads*

Input the following code when prompted: **7SH4N356FP**

For more information, turn to page 4

Acknowledgements

Published by Rockschool Ltd. © 2012, 2018 & 2020
Catalogue Number: RSK200067US
ISBN: 978-1-78936-163-6
Initial US Release | Errata details can be found at *www.rslawards.com/errata*

CONTACTING ROCKSCHOOL
www.rslawards.com
Telephone: +44 (0)345 460 4747
Email: *info@rslawards.com*

Syllabus Designer
Nik Preston

Producer
Nik Preston

Syllabus Advisor and Project Management
Sharon Kelly

Proof reading
Sharon Kelly, Jono Harrison, Nik Preston (and all arrangers/performers)

Syllabus Consultants (Hit Tunes 2018 Repertoire)
Guitar: James Betteridge, Andy G Jones
Bass: Joe Hubbard, Diego Kovadloff, Joel McIver
Drums: Paul Elliott, Pete Riley

Arrangers (Hit Tunes 2018 Repertoire)
Guitar: James Betteridge, Andy G Jones, Mike Goodman, Viv Lock
Bass: Diego Kovadloff, Andy Robertson, Joe Hubbard
Drums: Paul Elliott, Stu Roberts, Pete Riley

Publishing (Hit Tunes 2018 Repertoire)
Fact files by Diego Kovadloff
Covers designed by Phil Millard (Rather Nice design)
Music engraving, internal design and layout by
Simon Troup & Jennie Troup (Digital Music Art)

Distribution
Exclusive Distributors: Hal Leonard

Musicians (Hit Tunes 2018 Repertoire)
Guitar: Andy G Jones, James Betteridge, Mike Goodman, David Rhodes (Peter Gabriel)
Bass: Nik Preston, Joe Hubbard, Stuart Clayton, Andy Robertson, John Illsley (Dire Straits)
Drums: Paul Elliott, Pete Riley, Peter Huntington, Stu Roberts, Billy Cobham (Miles Davis, Mahavishnu Orchestra)
Vocals: Kim Chandler
Keys: Jono Harrison, Hannah V (on 'Red Baron'), Andy Robertson
Horns: Tom Walsh (tpt), Martin Williams (sax), Andy Wood (trmb)

Endorsements (Hit Tunes 2018 Repertoire)
Nik Preston: Overwater basses, Positive Grid amps
Paul Elliott: Liberty drums, Istanbul Mehmet cymbals, Regal Tip drumsticks, Remo heads, ACS custom ear plugs, Protection Racket cases
Stu Roberts: Paiste cymbals, Regal Tip drumsticks, Yamaha drums, Protection Racket cases

Recording & Audio Engineering (Hit Tunes 2018 Repertoire)
Recording engineers: Oli Jacobs, Scott Barnett, Patrick Phillips
Mixing engineer: Samuel Vasanth
Mastering engineer: Samuel Vasanth
Audio production: Nik Preston
Audio management: Ash Preston, Samuel Vasanth
Recording studios: Real World Studios, The Premises

Publishing (Rockschool 2012 Repertoire)
Fact Files written by Joe Bennett, Charlie Griffiths, Stephen Lawson, Simon Pitt, Stuart Ryan and James Uings
Walkthroughs written by James Uings
Music engraving, internal design and layout by
Simon Troup & Jennie Troup (Digital Music Art)
Proof reading and copy editing by Chris Bird, Claire Davies, Stephen Lawson, Simon Pitt and James Uings
Publishing administration by Caroline Uings
Additional drum proof reading by Miguel Andrews

Instrumental Specialists (Rockschool 2012 Repertoire)
Guitar: James Uings
Bass: Stuart Clayton
Drums: Noam Lederman

Musicians (Rockschool 2012 Repertoire)
Andy Crompton, Camilo Tirado, Carl Sterling, Charlie Griffiths, Chris Webster, Dave Marks, DJ Harry Love, Felipe Karam, Fergus Gerrand, Henry Thomas, Jake Painter, James Arben, James Uings, Jason Bowld, Joe Bennett, Jon Musgrave, Kishon Khan, Kit Morgan, Larry Carlton, Neel Dhorajiwala, Nir Z, Noam Lederman, Norton York, Richard Pardy, Ross Stanley, Simon Troup, Steve Walker, Stuart Clayton, Stuart Ryan

Endorsements (Rockschool 2012 Repertoire)
Noam Lederman: Mapex drums, Paiste cymbals, Vic Firth Sticks

Recording & Audio Engineering (Rockschool 2012 Repertoire)
Recorded at The Farm (Fisher Lane Studios)
Produced and engineered by Nick Davis
Assistant engineer and Pro Tools operator Mark Binge
Mixed and mastered at Langlei Studios
Mixing and additional editing by Duncan Jordan
Supporting Tests recorded by Duncan Jordan and Kit Morgan
Mastered by Duncan Jordan
Executive producers: James Uings, Jeremy Ward and Noam Lederman

Executive Producers
John Simpson, Norton York

RSL Awarding the Contemporary Arts

Table of Contents

Introductions & Information

Hit Tunes

Rockschool Originals

Technical Exercises

Supporting Tests

Additional Information

Welcome to Rockschool Drums Level/Grade 7

Welcome to Drums Level/Grade 7

Welcome to the **Rockschool 2018 Drums syllabus**. This book and the accompanying downloadable audio contain everything you need to play drums at this level/grade. In the book you will find the assessment scores in standard drum notation, as well as Fact Files and Walkthroughs for each song.

The downloadable audio includes:

- full stereo mixes of six Rockschool compositions and six arrangements of classic and contemporary hits
- backing tracks (in both click and no-click versions, minus the assessed drum part)
- all necessary audio for the complete range of supporting tests

Drum Assessments

At each level/grade, you have the option of taking one of two different types of assessment:

- **Level/Grade Assessment:** a Level/Grade Assessment is a mixture of music performances, technical work and tests. You prepare three pieces (two of which may be Free Choice Pieces) and the contents of the Technical Exercise section. This accounts for 75% of the assessment marks. The other 25% consists of a Quick Study Piece (10%), a pair of instrument specific Ear Tests (10%), and finally you will be asked five General Musicianship Questions (5%). The pass mark is 60%.

- **Performance Certificate:** in a Performance Certificate you play five pieces. Up to three of these can be Free Choice Pieces. Each song is marked out of 20 and the pass mark is 60%.

Book Contents

The book is divided into a number of sections. These are:

- **Assessment Pieces:** in this book you will find six specially commissioned pieces of Level/Grade 7 standard. Each of these is preceded by a ***Fact File***. Each Fact File contains a summary of the song, its style, tempo, key and technical features, along with a list of the musicians who played on it. The song itself is printed on up to four pages. Immediately after each song is a ***Walkthrough***. This covers the song from a performance perspective, focusing on the technical issues you will encounter. Each song comes with a full mix version and a backing track. Both versions have spoken count-ins at the beginning. Please note that any solos played on the full mix versions are indicative only.

- **Technical Exercises:** you should prepare the exercises set in this level/grade in the keys indicated. You should also choose ***one*** Stylistic Study from the three printed to practise and play to the backing track in the assessment. The style you choose will determine the style of the Quick Study Piece.

- **Supporting Tests and General Musicianship Questions:** in Drums Level/Grade 7 there are three supporting tests – a Quick Study Piece, a pair of Ear Tests and a set of General Musicianship Questions (GMQs) asked at the end of each assessment. Examples of the types of tests likely to appear in the assessment are printed in this book. Additional examples of both types of test and the GMQs can be found in the Rockschool *Companion Guide to Drums*.

- **Additional Information:** finally, you will find information on assessment procedures and marking schemes.

Audio

Audio is provided in the form of backing tracks (minus drums, and in two versions: click and no-click) and examples (including drums) for the pieces and the supporting tests where applicable. Audio files are supplied in MP3 format to enable playback on a wide range of compatible devices. Digital versions of the book include audio files in the download. Download audio for hardcopy books from RSL directly at *www.rslawards.com/downloads* — you will need to input this code when prompted: **7SH4N356FP**

Syllabus Guide

All candidates should read the accompanying syllabus guide when using this level/grade book. This can be downloaded from the RSL website: *www.rslawards.com*

Errata

Updates and changes to Rockschool books are documented online. Candidates should check for errata periodically while studying for any assessment. Further details can be found on the RSL website: *www.rslawards.com/errata*

Mary J Blige

SONG TITLE: FAMILY AFFAIR
ALBUM: NO MORE DRAMA
LABEL: MCA
GENRE: DANCE POP / HIP-HOP / R&B

WRITTEN BY: MARY J. BLIGE, ANDRE YOUNG, BRUCE MILLER, CAMARA KAMBON, MICHAEL ELIZONDO
PRODUCED BY: DR. DRE

US CHART PEAK: 1

BACKGROUND INFO

'Family Affair' was originally written by Dr. Dre, who recorded its initial instrumental version in September 2000. He sent the track to Mary J. Blige who recorded her vocals using lyrics written by her brother, Bruce Miller, in collaboration with Camara Kambon and Michael Elizondo. The song was originally titled 'Fragile'. Dr.Dre suggested adding a bridge to the song and Blige did so, for which she penned her own lyrics.

The song's pumping dance-pop incorporated elements of hip-hop and R&B. This is a mix characteristic of Mary J. Blige's sound, for which she is regarded as highly influential. It became the blueprint for much of 90s hip-hop and R&B. 'Family Affair' topped the Billboard Hot 100 charts for six weeks. It is amongst the biggest selling songs in the Billboard Hot 100 All-Time Songs. Blige performed the song at the final night of the Democratic National Convention in 2012.

One of the drummers associated with Mary J. Blige is Gerald Heyward – he ranks amongst the most respected players in the R&B world, and has also worked with Beyoncé, Michael Jackson, Puff Daddy, Missy Elliott and Coolio.

Mary J. Blige's career has seen her work with a who's who of the R&B and pop worlds. She has been touring since 1997. Amongst her collaborators in R&B and hip-hop are Dr. Dre, Will.i.am, Raphael Saadiq, LL Cool J, Jimmy Jam, R. Kelly, Puff Daddy and Kanye West. In the pop world she has collaborated with George Michael by recording 'As' by Stevie Wonder – this was huge commercial and critical success. She also duetted with Barbra Streisand, Jessie J, Emeli Sandé, Sam Smith, Sting and Chaka Khan, earning her first Grammy Award for her work with the latter. She has been awarded two Grammy Awards to date.

Mary J. Blige has also been a very busy film actor, with parts in *Prison Dog*, *I Can Do Bad All By Myself*, *Rock Of Ages*, *Black Nativity*, *Mudbound* and *Sherlock Holmes*. She has also had many TV appearances as actress, guest and judge. She is also an entrepreneur with her own record label, production company, perfume and sunglasses collection.

Mary J. Blige is a vocal supporter of the Democratic Party and an example of entrepreneurship to many. She has been a leading figure in popular music for the best part of two decades.

Family Affair

Mary J Blige

Words & Music by Mary J. Blige, Bruce Miller, Andre Young,
Melvin Bradford, Mike Elizondo, Camara Kambon, Asiah Louis & Luchana Lodge

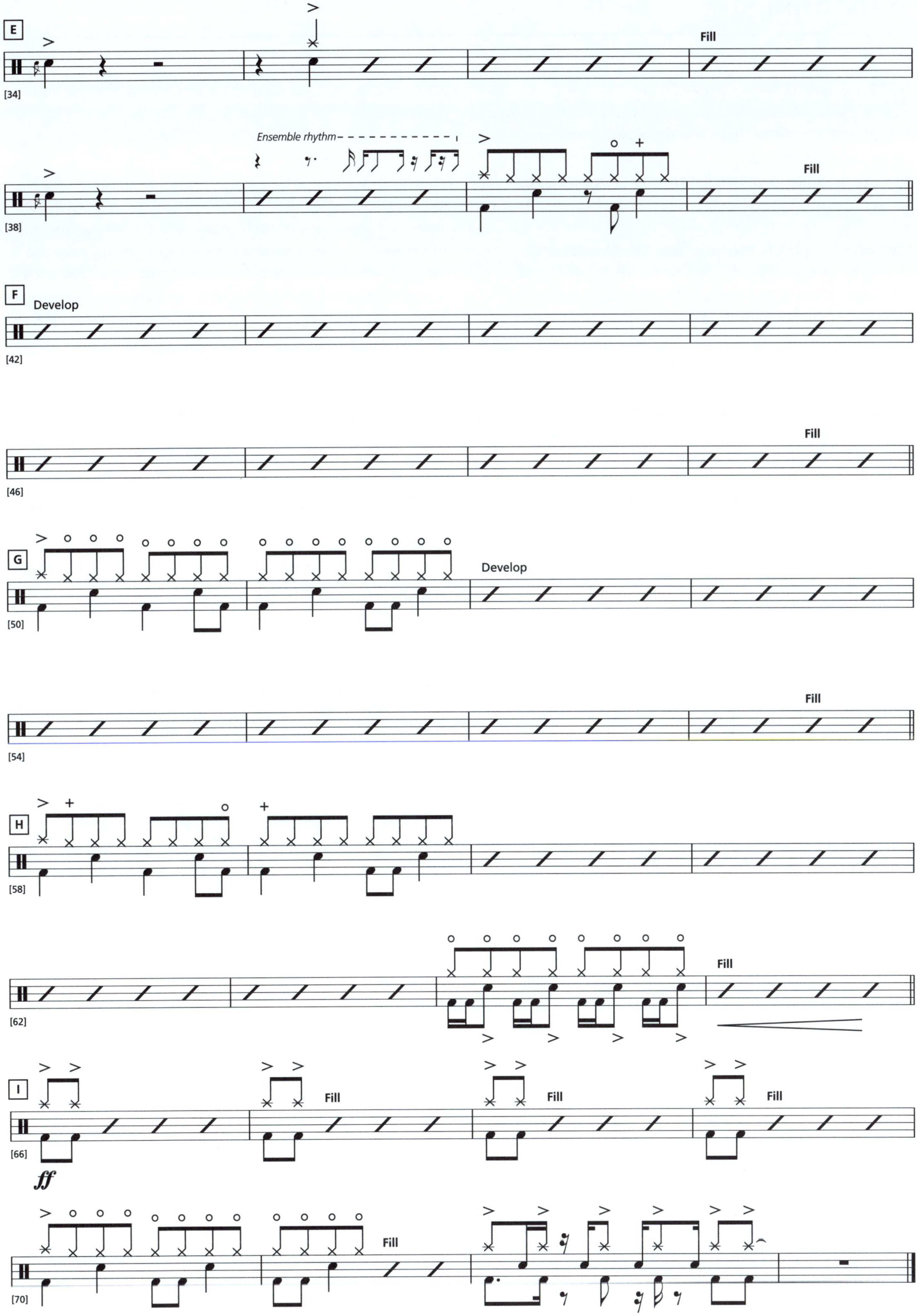
E
Fill
[34]
Ensemble rhythm
Fill
[38]
F
Develop
[42]
Fill
[46]
G
Develop
[50]
Fill
[54]
H
[58]
Fill
[62]
I
Fill
Fill
Fill
[66]
ff
Fill
[70]

Walkthrough

Arrangement Considerations

At first glance the shortened arrangement of Family Affair may appear simple, perhaps too simple for Level/Grade 7. However, to paraphrase the renowned drum teacher Stanley Spector, "often in drumming, the simplest lesson is the most advanced – time!"

Measures 1–3 | *Introduction fill and two-measure loop*
The first measure utilises flams on the snare drum and syncopated bass drum figures. Play this figure with confidence as it introduces the song. The drum part on the original recording consists of a two-measure rhythmic loop in 4/4 at 93 beats per minute. There is no dynamic or rhythmic change throughout the song. In this arrangement the drum part has been adapted to create a "live" feel. The essence of the two-measure pattern is the same but there is increased rhythmic colour.

General Groove Considerations

The Hi-Hat
The hi-hat part consists of eighth notes throughout. Consider how to phrase these notes. Experiment with accenting every note or perhaps the first of every group of two, accenting the backbeat or playing with no accent at all. Choose the option which suits the music the most. Try to think with a record producer's mindset and find the sound that works best in context.

Snare Drum Articulation
The snare drum plays a consistent backbeat which does not deviate at any point. Remember every backbeat should sound the same. There should be no fluctuations in timbre or dynamic volume. Experiment with playing a rim-shot or playing in the centre of the drum with the tip of the stick. A rim-shot occurs when the drum is struck in the centre of the head at the same time as the shaft of the stick strikes the drum rim. Striking the rim causes the shell to vibrate and thus creates a sharper sound and greater volume. Think about stick grip and position. If you are playing using matched grip are you playing in French, German or American hand positions? Think about how these different hand positions produce different tones. A small change of hand position can make a big difference in sound. Choose the technique which allows the snare drum to sit comfortably within the internal dynamics of the drum kit.

Bass Drum Articulation
When playing this groove think about the internal dynamics. How loud are the relative volumes between the bass drum and snare? Does the bass drum have a soft initial attack or is it more staccato? Should the bass drum beater play into the head or off the head? There are no correct answers. Ultimately, the candidate must play the groove in a way which brings together all of their drumming abilities and musical taste.

Measure 10 | *Eight-measure sections*
This song is composed entirely of sections which are eight measures in length, apart from the outro. An experienced drummer should know their location in the arrangement at all times. It is recommended the candidate memorises the song form as it is easy to get lost when playing a constantly repetitive figure. Listen to the backing track for any musical clues from the other instruments which will provide musical landmarks during the performance.

Measures 18 and 34 | *Stop time figures*
There are stop time measures where the rhythm section breaks the constant rhythm. This creates interest in the arrangement. Both measures feature a flam on beat 1 – a dramatic musical statement as the snare usually plays on the second beat. In measure 34 there is a longer gap before the band come back in. The entry on beat 2 of measure 35 creates even more tension.

Measure 39 | *Ensemble figure*
After another flam stop time in measure 38 the band enters again with a syncopated ensemble figure. The candidate should orchestrate this rhythm in a way which suits the music, by playing the figure only or adding additional ornaments. The candidate should experiment with various voicings and deliver a well-thought-out concept in the assessment.

Measure 42 | *Develop*
Time slashes with "Develop" written above are used at measure 42. These measures occur throughout the arrangement. The aim is to develop your part, responding to the dynamic and feel of the band around you, just as you would in a live context. This is the candidate's opportunity to shine, playing musically appropriate ideas which complement the music.

Measure 64 | *Double time figure*
At measure 64 the arranger has included a double time rhythmic figure. This means that the back beat doubles its rate and becomes the off-beat eighth note. Enjoy the double strokes on the bass drum and play these with clarity.

Measure 66 | *Hits and solo fills*
From measure 66 there are four measures of rhythmic hits on the first two eighth notes of each measure. It's worth developing fills and dynamic excitement in-between these figures, leading into the final two measures of rhythm and the syncopated 16th-note figure in the penultimate measure. Pay attention to phrasing with the band. Enjoy this challenging piece which contains lots of scope for dynamic change and improvisation.

Tower of Power

SONG TITLE: WHAT IS HIP?
ALBUM: TOWER OF POWER
LABEL: ARISTA/BMG
GENRE: SOUL FUNK / JAZZ FUNK

WRITTEN BY: EMILIO CASTILLO, STEPHEN KUPKA AND DAVID GARIBALDI
PRODUCED BY: TOWER OF POWER

US CHART PEAK: 91

BACKGROUND INFO

'What Is Hip?' is the opening track on Tower Of Power's 1973 eponymous album, it was their third studio release and their most successful album to date. It peaked at no.15 on the Billboard Top LPs chart and sold over half a million copies. 'What Is Hip?' made the Billboard Hot 100.

Tower Of Power was formed in Oakland in 1968 by tenor saxophonist and vocalist Emilio Castillo and baritone saxophonist Stephen Kupka. From the onset the band appealed to minority and rebellious listeners. Their brand of fiery soul developed hand in hand with their popular and legendary live performances. Tower Of Power's contribution to the sound of funk and soul is very significant. Borrowing from early funk, soul and motown influences, they managed to carve a highly original and identifiable sound. By the mid 1970s Tower of Power were a highly respected band in the US.

The driving rhythm section of David Garibaldi on drums and Rocco Prestia on bass propelled the soulful vocals of Lenny Williams, who replaced Rufus Miller at the time of recording *Tower Of Power*. A young Lenny Pickett joined the band as lead saxophonist for the recording, adding to what would become a legendary horn section in the business. After various line up changes, including over 60 musicians in over 40 years of live and studio performance, Tower Of Power managed to retain their unique and singular sound.

David Garibaldi is regarded as a drummer of enormous significance in the funk and soul worlds. His pocket playing and intricate hi-hat and ghost note work are at the centre of a driving and complimentary style that made his drumming a pivotal reference. His innovative linear drumming concepts are testament to a highly developed sense of musicality. David Garibaldi is a dedicated educator and has published many acclaimed books and videos that explain his approach in detail. Besides his work with Tower Of Power, Dave Garibaldi has worked with a number of top tier artists including Patti Austin, Natalie Cole, Larry Carlton, Jermaine Jackson, Ray Obiedo, Boz Scaggs, The Buddy Rich Orchestra, Gino Vannelli and The Yellowjackets.

Tower Of Power released 11 albums, including two live records, between 1970 and 1981. More recordings followed from 1986 onwards, together with many tours worldwide. They are still active and performing their unique brand of funk and soul.

What Is Hip

Tower of Power

Words & Music by David Garibaldi, Stephen Kupka & Emilio Castillo

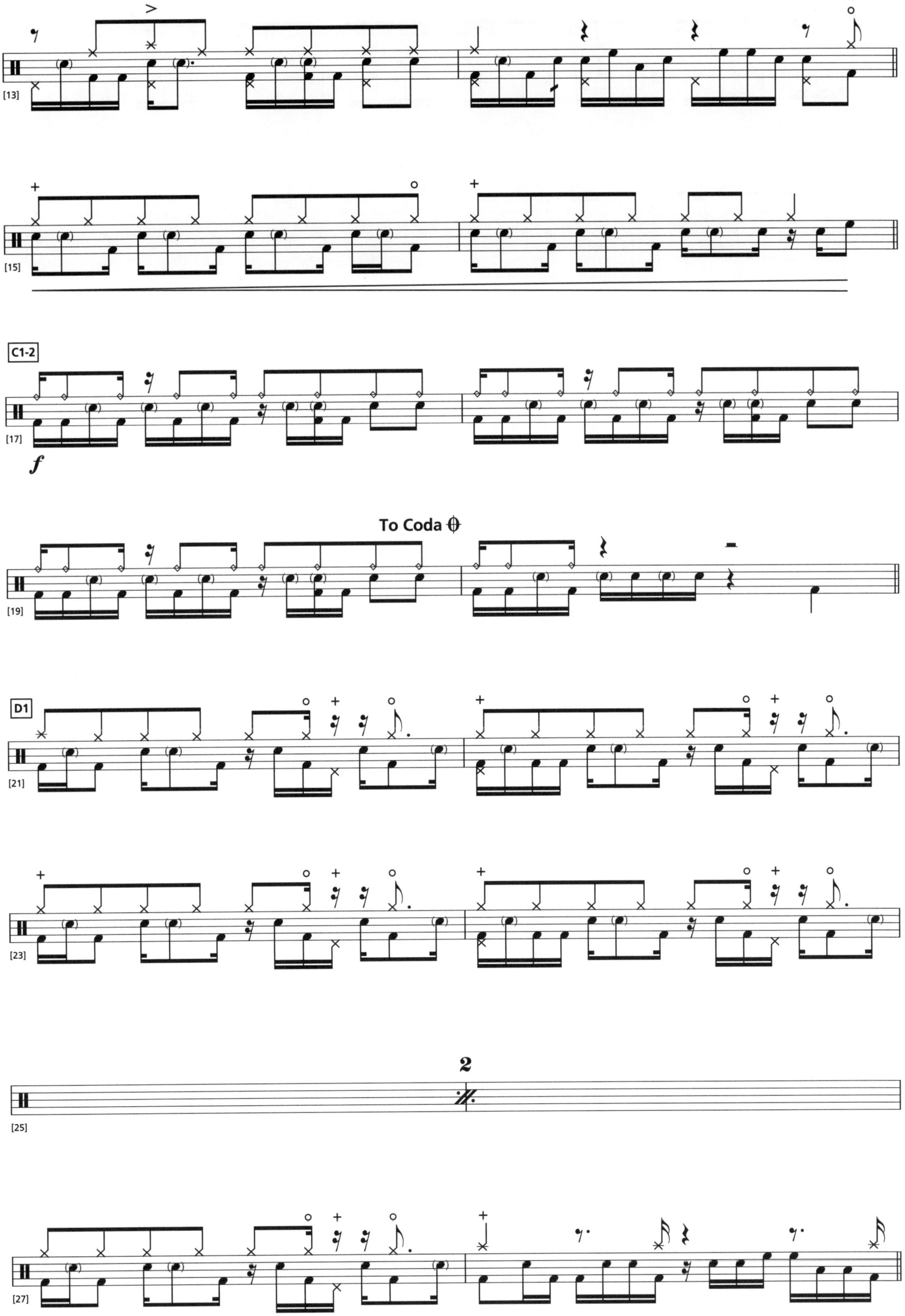
[13]
[15]
C1-2
[17]
f
To Coda
[19]
D1
[21]
[23]
2
[25]
[27]

Intro 2
[29]
[31]
Fill
D.%. al Coda
Coda
[33]
[35]
[37]
[39]
Organ Solo
[41]
mf
[43]

[45]
[47]
[49]
f
cont. sim.
[51]
D2
[53]
[55]
[57]
[59]

Walkthrough

This piece features challenging grooves which require a high degree of control and independence. One of the fundamental requirements is playing all ghosted snare drum notes as quietly as possible. Without this delicate touch the contrast between the ghost notes and backbeats will be lost.

Intro

The piece begins with a one-beat fill, played as single-strokes, which ends with the left hand playing the final 16th note of the measure on an open hi-hat. The hi-hats are then closed on beat 1 of the next measure which features the first of several challenging grooves in this piece. The pattern is made up of a broken 16th-note rhythm on the hi-hats with a layered left hand ghost note pattern played beneath. Notice that the left foot also steps quarter-notes which creates the open hi-hat on the last 16th note of each beat.

A Section 1–2 (Measure 3)

The A section features a slightly different pattern to that seen during the intro. Firstly the right hand rhythm features a more broken pattern while the left foot is only stepping two and four, which generates an open hi-hat on the last 16th note of beats 1 and 3. The left hand also accents the second 16th note of beat 3 as well as beats 2 and 4.

B Section 1–2 (Measure 11)

The B section moves the right hand over to the ride cymbal as well as featuring crashes which appear a beat later than expected, landing on beat 2. The left hand also maintains ghost notes in many of the 16th note spaces.

Measure 12

The fill on beat 2 of measure 12 should be played as single-strokes so the crash will be played in the left hand. The fill on beat 4 could be played leading with either hand but is probably easiest if played leading with the left hand so the right hand plays the last 16th note of the measure on the open hi-hats.

Measure 15

Hit the first note hard and then drop dynamically in order to gradually build over this and the next measure. The left hand fills in the second 16th note of each beat as a ghost note.

C Section 1–2 (Measure 17)

With the dynamics building to forte, letter C features a Latin-esque pattern played on the bell of the ride. Watch for the layering of notes on beat 3 as this can be challenging to execute. Beat 2 of measure 20 should ideally be played leading with the left hand so the right moves down from the ride cymbal to play the accented upbeat 16th notes.

D Section (Measure 21)

Letter D features another challenging groove. It's a two-measure pattern that has a syncopated open hi-hat figure towards the end of each measure that's made all more the challenging by the hi-hats being open for different durations; on the '&' of beat 3 they're open for a 16th-note duration whereas on the second 16th note of beat 4 they remain open for a dotted eighth-note duration and until beat 1 of the next measure.

Measure 28

The fill at the end of measure 28 is ideally played leading with the right hand so that, despite starting on the upbeat 16th note, the final crash is played in the right hand.

Intro 2 (Measure 29)

Measure 29 returns to the original intro feel for four measures with the final measure featuring a fill to set up the syncopated hits in the beats 3 and 4. In measure 32 is the indication to ***D.S. al Coda*** which means heading back to the 'S' sign in measure 3 and playing through until the ***Coda*** sign in measure 19.

Coda (Measure 19)

The ***Coda*** appears on the third measure of the C section whilst playing the Latin-style bell pattern. Half way through this measure the right hand should move over to the hi-hats ready to hit the upbeat 16th notes and the final 16th note of the measure on the open hi-hat.

D Section 1 (Measure 33)

Measure 33 is essentially built around the right hand playing upbeat 16th note punctuations, an approach which should continue through measures 38 and 39 where the last three 16th notes of each beat should be played right, left, right.

Measure 41

The first measure of the organ solo is a deceptive one. On first listen it could be assumed to be a one-measure fill. However, it is in fact the first measure of an eight-measure section that is orchestrated around the kit, as opposed to the linear-style groove that follows. The hi-tom and hi-hats in measure 41 should all be played with the right hand.

Measure 42

This is another challenging pattern which can be difficult to play smoothly. Like all of the grooves within this piece, it's dependent upon the ghost notes being played quietly and may benefit from slow practice and working it up to speed.

Measure 49

The right hand moves from the hi-hats to the ride cymbal in measure 49 and for the next four measures.

D2 (Measure 53)

D2 is essentially the same as D1 with the same patterns, upbeat 16th-note anticipations and leads through to the final crashes which end the piece.

Richard Spaven

SONG TITLE: LAW
ALBUM: THE SELF
LABEL: FINE LINE / SOUL HAS NO TEMPO
GENRE: ELECTRONIC SOUL / DRUM 'N' BASS

WRITTEN BY: RICHARD SPAVEN AND STUART MCCALLUM
PRODUCED BY: RICHARD SPAVEN

US CHART PEAK: N/A

♩=160 *Atmospheric Jungle / Drum'n'Bass*

Intro

BACKGROUND INFO

'Law' is a single release from Richard Spaven's second solo album *The Self*. The track is a haunting and atmospheric instrumental featuring Spaven on drums and his long time collaborator Stuart McCallum on guitar. 'Law' is characteristic of Spaven's approach to drumming and composition. His atmospheric tracks blend a harmonically rich palette with elements of ambient sounds, which allow for intricate and interesting drumming that, whilst prominent, still serve the song.

Richard Spaven is a highly sought after and respected drummer. His fluid technique and light touch project his style as a bridge between jazz and electronica in a dexterous and musically rich fashion. His compositions on *The Self* blend jazz drumming with club music in an organic and genre defying way. The record features elements of drum and bass, broken beat, dubstep and collaborations with the likes of Cleveland Watkiss, Kris Bowers, Jameszoo and Jordan Rakei with whom he also recorded 'Toko', featured on Rakei's highly acclaimed *Cloak*.

Richard Spaven has worked with artists including The Cinematic Orchestra, José James, Guru's Jazzmatazz, Flying Lotus, Gregory Porter and TY. His trademark drumming, blending precision and finesse are matched by a unique production style. Richard Spaven is also a well known clinician with engagements all over the world. He is an endorsee of Vic Firth drumsticks, Meinl cymbals and Yamaha drums.

Law

Richard Spaven

Words & Music by Richard Spaven & Stuart McCallum

[33]
[36]
[39]
[42]
B
[45]
f
[48]
[51]
[54]
[57]
[60]

[63]
[66]
Drum Break
[69]
[71]
C
[73]
[76]
[79]
[82]
[85]
[88]

[91]
[93]
[96]
[99]
[102]
D
[105]
mf
[108]
2
2
[111]
Outro
[113]
mp
[116]

Walkthrough

Richard Spaven's 'Law' features an uptempo drum 'n' bass style feel throughout. The main component to convey this feel is the anticipated backbeat on the '&' of beat 3 as opposed to the customary beat 4. In addition to this syncopation there's a liberal use of ghost notes which really need to be played as quietly as possible (about one inch off the drum) to convey the desired sound. The key to look for here is getting the ghost notes to blend with the sound of the hi-hat.

Intro and A Section (Measures 1–44)

The drums enter after the twelve-measure intro. Notice how in measure 13 the groove starts on beat 2, leaving beat 1 completely empty. This is a theme that appears throughout the track, effectively working as a deceptive cadence, where the listener expects something to appear or resolve at a certain point but it has instead been moved.

The main groove that appears through section A is essentially the same drum 'n' bass inspired pattern that runs through the whole piece, with the key component being the second backbeat of the measure being played an eighth-note early on the '&' of beat 3.

Measures 16–17 and 24–25

An open hi-hat is played on the last eighth-note of measure 16 and not then closed until beat 2 of the following measure. Holding the hi-hats open over the bar line gives a feeling of the time being suspended, as again the listener is anticipating something on the downbeat of the next measure. This same idea appears in measures 24 and 25.

Measure 44

The transition into letter B is notable as measure 44 would traditionally be a place to play a fill and alert the listener to the impending change, but instead the drums essentially stop with a snare/cymbal crash on beat 1 and are followed by a two-beat rhythm played on the hi-hats. Notice again how a traditional crash on the downbeat of measure 45 is omitted with the drums instead rejoining on beat 2.

B Section (Measures 45–72)

Letter B is a 24 measure section where the groove is the same throughout, except for measure 1 with its missing downbeat. You may also notice the lift in dynamics to forte.

Measure 69

There's a four-measure drum break which starts in measure 69. Measures 69 and 70 are the same but in measure 71 an over-the-barline dotted quarter-note based figure is played on the snare whilst the right hand maintains eighth-notes on the hi-hats. Measures 71 and 72 are probably best practised as a two-measure pattern to develop this phrase.

C Section (Measures 73–104)

Measure 73 is the start of the C section which is 32 measures long and features the recurring theme of crashing beat 2 instead of beat 1 of each four-measure phrase. Another theme which occurs several times in this section is half-time, where the regular backbeat is moved to beat 3. This can be seen in measures 76, 80 and 84. This section concludes with the snare playing another dotted quarter-note over-the-barline figure starting from beat 3 of measure 101 all the way to measure 104. Here the left hand is in fact playing a dotted eighth-note rhythm but accenting every other note to outline the dotted quarter-note.

D Section (Measures 105–112)

Letter D and measure 105 sees a drop in dynamics back to mezzo forte and settles into the two-measure pattern which can be seen in measures 107 and 108.

Outro (Measures 113–119)

There's another drop in dynamics to mezzo piano at measure 113 along with a transition to cross-stick. At first glance it looks like the same hand pattern is played from measures 113 to 118 but look out for the earlier placement of the backbeat on the '&' of beat 1 in measure 116. Notice also that the final crash is played on its own with no accompanying bass drum.

Chase & Status

SONG TITLE: CONTROL
ALBUM: TRIBE
LABEL: JIVE
GENRE: DRUM AND BASS / ELECTRONIC / DANCEHALL

WRITTEN BY: CHRISTIAN DYAS, MATTHEW GOODMAN, ISAAC HOLAMAN, WILL KENNARD, SAUL MILTON, PHILIP STANTON, LAURIE VINCENT, CHRISTOPHER WINK
PRODUCED BY: CHASE & STATUS

US CHART PEAK: N/A

♩=140 *Industrial Electronica*

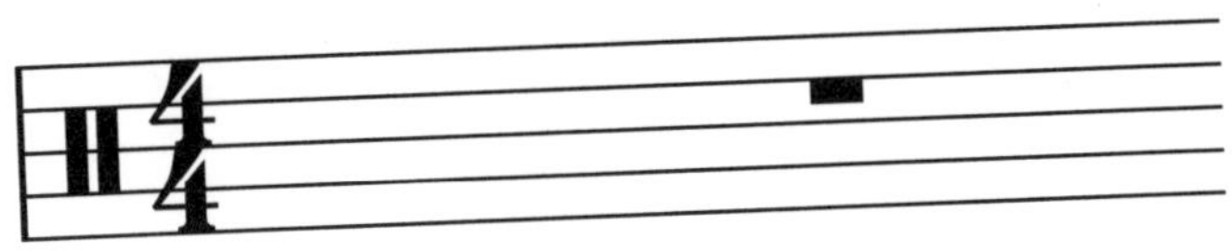

BACKGROUND INFO

'Control' is featured on *Tribe*, Chase & Status' fourth album, released in 2017. The record features their drum and bass style of old mixed with dancehall and grime influences and all was written collaboratively.

Chase & Status are two producers, Saul Milton and Will Kennard, who met at university. They are complimented by MC Rage and drummer Andy Gangadeen. The duo has achieved great success in the UK Dance charts, reaching the no. 1 spot three times, with 'Hurt You / Sell Me Your Soul' in 2007, with 'Take Me Away / Judgement (Informer)' in 2008, and with 'Pieces' featuring Plan B also in 2008.

Chase & Status also had great success in the UK Single charts reaching no.1 with 'End Credits' featuring Plan B and 'No More Idols' featuring Mali on vocals. Other successful singles include 'Hypest Hype', a digital release featuring Tinie Tempah, 'Blind Faith' featuring soul singer and songwriter Liam Bailey, 'Time' featuring Delilah, 'Hitz', featuring Tinie Tempah and 'Heavy' featuring Dizzee Rascal. Chase & Status' second album, *No More Idols*, reached no. 2 in the UK albums Chart and was certified gold.

Chase & Status are a powerful live act and drummer Andy Gangadeen plays a central role in it. Whilst performances include an element of improvisation or embellishment, Gangadeen delivers meticulously planned parts, triggering a variety of sounds and loops that, in combination with his precise drumming, create an exciting and powerful live performance. Andy Gangadeen is no stranger to the live scene. He is a long established drummer with impeccable credentials including recording and performing with many successful artists such as the Spice Girls, Massive Attack, Jeff Beck, The Bays, Duran Duran and M People.

'Control' sees Chase & Status delve into territory opened by The Prodigy in the early 1990s. Neo punk band Slaves joined them for the track. Other collaborations featured on *Tribe* include 'Reload' with Craig David and 'Love Me More' with Emeli Sandé. As part of their in-demand production work the duo has remixed The Prodigy and produced for artists including Rihanna, Rita Ora and Alexandra Burke. Other remix credits include Dizzee Rascal, Nneka and Capleton.

Control

Chase & Status

Words & Music by Saul Milton, William Kennard, Matthew Goldman,
Philip Stanton, Christian Dyas, Christopher Wink, Isaac Holman & Lawrence Vincent

C
[25]
f
[29]
D
[33]
[36]
[39]
E
[41]
ff
[44]
etc.
[47]

F
[49]
[52]
2
[55]
Fill
G
Stick on stick
[57]
mf
[61]
H
[65]
f
[69]
I
[73]

[76]
[79]
Fill
J
[81]
ff
[84]
[87]
K
[89]
[92]
2
[95]
Fill

Walkthrough

Measure 5 | *Stick on stick technique*
This exciting piece begins with the drummer playing eighth-notes using stick on stick technique. Hold one drumstick static and strike it with the other one. Remember to accent every other eighth note to create intensity in the rhythm. The dynamic is mezzo-forte. Play with conviction and avoid holding the sticks too tight as this will dampen the sound.

Measure 6 | *One-measure repeat*
A one-measure repeat sign is used in measure 6. This simply means repeat the previous measure. One-measure repeats are frequently used in rhythm section charts. The one-measure repeat is used throughout.

Measure 8 | *Drum fill sticking*
An unusual change in voicing occurs in measure 8. There is a rapid movement to change from stick on stick to the snare drum for the last two 16th notes of beat 3. Tonal variation is also created by the high tom and floor tom eighth-notes on beat 4. Hands must move quickly to get back to the stick on stick rhythm which continues from measure 9.

Measure 17 | *Ride cymbal intensity*
The eighth note rhythm transfers onto the ride cymbal while the bass drum plays quarter notes from measure 17. Playing all four quarter notes on the bass drum is sometimes called "four on the floor". This texture is used at various points in the arrangement.

Measure 21 | *Four-measure crescendo*
The tension builds at measure 21 as a crescendo begins. Remember to leave enough dynamic headroom to achieve this crescendo when playing the previous section which is at a lower dynamic. At the end of measure 24 there is a strong voicing of both snare, bass drum and floor tom together for the final two eighth-notes.

Measure 25 | *Hi-hat 16th-notes*
16th notes begin at measure 25 where single sticking is recommended. Play these accurately at this fast tempo accenting the first of every four notes. The dynamic is forte so don't hold back but take into account how loud the backing track is and also any dynamic changes later in the arrangement. When accenting the hi-hat make sure that the bass drum is playing at exactly the same time and there are no flams between voices. The candidate should feel free to develop the hi-hat part after establishing the pattern.

Measure 37 | *Crash cymbal intensity*
Intensity builds in the song and the drums add to the fray by adding additional crashes. These crashes increase in use and appear every two beats in measures 37 and 38. The compositional term for an increase in use or a shortening in rhythmic value is diminution.

Measure 39 | *Two-measure drum fill*
A great drum fill finishes this intense section. Thunderous 16th notes on the snare drum are super-imposed with three over four rhythmic accents. The accent pattern is exactly what would appear if a dotted quarter note was played repeatedly for the first five quarter note beats. The arranger has also added the bass drum to mark out the accent pattern. There is further tonal variation on beats 2 and 3 where the high tom and floor tom play a linear combination. Single sticking for beat 2 and paradiddle sticking for beat 3 is recommended.

Measure 41 | *Groove change*
A heavily syncopated groove is used for eight measures starting at measure 41. Play this rhythm at the correct dynamic of Fortissimo and pay attention to the subtle rhythmic changes.

Measure 49 | *Half-time feel*
The time feel changes to a half-time feel at measure 49. Half time is a term referring to a heavy accent on beat 3 when the original tempo remains the same. At measure 55 the snare drum reverts to a standard backbeat but with a displacement on beat 3. As the song form repeats, many of these elements crop up again. Focus hard on consistency and accurate delivery throughout. There are some exciting moments in this challenging piece. Enjoy 'Control'.

Justin Timberlake

SONG TITLE: CRY ME A RIVER
ALBUM: JUSTIFIED
LABEL: JIVE
GENRE: DISCO/R&B

WRITTEN BY: JUSTIN TIMBERLAKE, TIMOTHY MOSLEY AND SCOTT STORCH
PRODUCED BY: TIMBALAND

US CHART PEAK: 3

BACKGROUND INFO

Justin Timberlake wrote 'Cry Me A River' as a reflection of his breakup with Britney Spears. It is the story of a brokenhearted man who tries to move away from his girlfriend who cheated on him. The song was produced by Timbaland and features vocal and string elements that give the arrangement a haunting nature. 'Cry Me A River' blends various elements of R&B with a lyrical vocal style.

'Cry Me a River' was a massive worldwide success. It peaked at no. 3 on the Billboard Hot 100 chart and the Billboard Top 40. Combined worldwide sales of the single neared three million. The video for the song was also a massive success with nearly 260 million views on YouTube alone.

Timbaland's production lends itself to effective live renditions of the song. Timberlake started playing 'Cry Me A River' live during the *Justified World Tour* in 2003. He continues to perform it to date.

Amongst the drummers associated with his live work is Brian Frasier-Moore whose credits include Jill Scott, Usher, Patti LaBelle, Bruce Parham, Ernie Sanders, Teddy Pendergrass, Backstreet Boys, Toni Braxton, Christina Aguilera, Janet Jackson, Madonna and Queen Latifah. He is equally comfortable in pop, jazz-funk, gospel and R&B. He is a musical director, producer and a Pearl endorsee.

Justin Timberlake is no stranger to fame having been a cast member in *The Mickey Mouse Club* alongside Britney Spears and Christina Aguilera. The latter would become a tour mate and the former his girlfriend. Timberlake's solo career began after a highly successful stint with boy band NSYNC, he was one of two lead singers together with JC Chasez. His career reached even further heights upon the release of his second album *FutureSex/LoveSounds*. Justin Timberlake counts Michael Jackson, Stevie Wonder, Prince, David Bowie, Michael Hutchence and David Byrne amongst his influences.

Justified was awarded a Grammy for Best Pop Vocal Album in 2004 – that is one of 10 Grammy awards Justin Timberlake has received to date. He is one of today's pop icons with album sales over 32 million, single sales over 56 million and sales of 70 million as a member of NSYNC, making him one of the best selling artists of the last two decades.

Cry Me A River

Justin Timberlake

Words & Music by Justin Timberlake,
Scott Storch & Tim Mosley

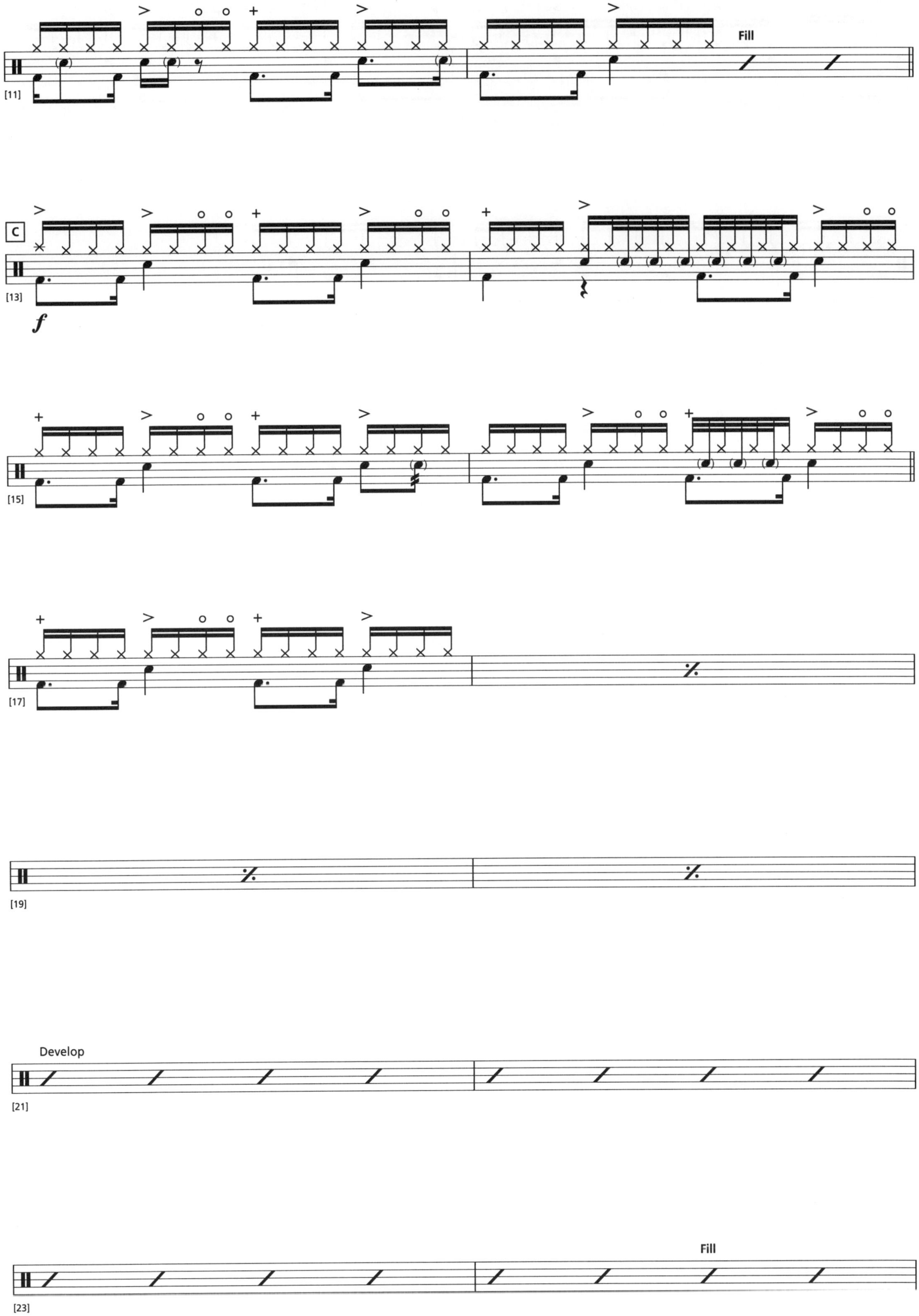
Fill
[11]
C
[13]
f
[15]
[17]
[19]
Develop
[21]
Fill
[23]

[25]
[27]
D
[29]
Fill
[31]
[33]
Develop
Fill
[35]
E
[37]

[39]
F
Develop
[41]
[43]
[45]
Fill
[47]
[49]
Fill
[51]
ff

Walkthrough

Measure 1 | *Introduction hi-hat sixteenth note pattern*
During the four-measure introduction the hi-hats are playing 16th notes. An accent is written above beats 2 and 4. Different sticking patterns will naturally create different phrasing. Try using alternating single sticking for these measures (R.L.R.L) and also using only the leading hand (R.R.R.R). Play the accents on the edge of the cymbals with the shaft of the stick and the unaccented notes on the surface area of the hi-hats. The dynamic is mezzo-piano and all internal dynamics are relevant to this. The bass drum plays the back beat, this can create some challenging co-ordination with the open and closed hi-hat syncopations.

Measure 4 | *Drum fill*
A complicated drum fill is used at the end of measure 5. The recommended sticking is to use inverted double strokes. The fill is largely linear in style and is a classic Steve Gadd influenced phrase. Play as accurately and as evenly as you can and be aware of the dynamics between each part of the drum kit. Enjoy this fill and learn it as a piece of drumming vocabulary.

Measure 5 | *Hi-hat technique*
The groove pattern contains hi-hat 16th notes. If technique allows, play these all with one hand. If this is beyond current technical ability, adapt the part by playing hand to hand single strokes. This will help simplify the part. When using only the leading hand on the hi-hats think about how to phrase. Play the accented notes on the edge of the cymbals and the unaccented notes with the tip of the stick on the surface of the cymbals. An accented stress on every other hi-hat note would bring out the eighth note rhythm. Another option is to accent only the quarter note and therefore group the hi-hat notes in fours. A third option is to accent the hi-hat on two and four and finally to play with no accent at all. Choose the pattern which suits the music the best.

Measure 5 | *Bass and snare drum*
In most contemporary music the bass drum and snare drum have a prominent place in the mix. The bass drum plays a dotted eighth note followed by a single 16th. This pattern repeats in the second half of the measure. Focus on consistency and accuracy and consider how loud the bass drum should be in relation to the other parts.

The snare drum plays a repetitive backbeat. Play the snare drum in the centre and experiment with different tones. Think about the internal dynamics of the groove. Consider whether to rim-shot. This is often subject to the tonal attack of the note that the drummer is trying to achieve, the tuning of the drum (including dampening), the room acoustics and so on. The drummer's role is to assess all of this information and play the part confidently with a good sound suitable for the performance environment.

Measure 12 | *Drum fill*
There are two time slashes used at the end of measure 12. This means play a fill over the last two beats. Choose a fill which fits the musical context and communicates the arrangement to the other musicians you are playing with.

Measure 14 | *32nd-note ghost-notes*
Use single sticking for these additional notes. Pay attention to the bass drum and make sure the rhythm isn't becoming lumpy in execution because of the additional thirty-second notes. Focus on dynamics and make sure the bracketed notes are very quiet.

Measure 32 | *Rhythm drop*
To complement vocal phrasing and create interest for the listener the rhythm drops out in places in measures 32 and 33. This creates interest and tension because until that point the rhythmic elements have been very repetitive.

Measure 42 | *Rhythm slashes*
Rhythm slashes are used from measure 42. The word develop is written above. Try different variations within the groove, paying attention to the style and musical environment.

Measure 49 | *Crash on beat 1*
The crash cymbal is used on occasion to extenuate the start of a musical section. In measure 49 the chorus has just begun.

Measure 52 | *Drum fill*
The fill in contains rudimental decoration with a snare drum flam. This is followed by tonal variation with the high tom and low tom playing 16th notes. Single sticking is recommended for this.

John Scofield

SONG TITLE: TECHNO
ALBUM: STILL WARM
LABEL: GRAMAVISION
GENRE: JAZZ FUSION

WRITTEN BY: JOHN SCOFIELD
PRODUCED BY: STEVE SWALLOW

US CHART PEAK: N/A

♩=130 *Jazz/Funk/Fusion*

Intro

BACKGROUND INFO

'Techno' is the opening track on John Scofield's highly acclaimed 1986 release *Still Warm*. For the recording John Scofield recruited keyboardist Don Grolnick, bassist Darryl Jones, and drummer Omar Hakim, with whom he worked in Miles Davis' group. *Still Warm* captures the essence of the mid 1980s Jazz Fusion sound.

John Scofield's influential guitar playing has been heard alongside some of the most highly respected jazz musicians in the world since he started out professionally in the early 1970s. He recorded and played with Charles Mingus, Miles Davis, Gary Burton, Steve Swallow, Mitchel Forman, Dennis Chambers, Peter Erskine, Bill Frisell, Charlie Haden, Joe Lovano, Jack DeJohnette, Pat Metheny, Bill Stewart, Idris Muhammad, Eddie Harris, Randy Brecker and composers Vince Mendoza and Mark-Anthony Turnage, amongst many others. Scofield is also an educator. His vast discography explores all corners of the jazz world and he is regarded as one of the most innovative guitarists in the field.

Omar Hakim began playing the drums aged 5. His father was a trombonist in Duke Ellington's and Count Basie's bands. Omar later studied with Clyde Lucas from Basie's band and had much contact with Elvin Jones and Art Blakey whom he got to know through his father's friendship with John Coltrane.

Hakim joined the legendary Weather Report aged 23 in 1982. Previously he worked with Mike Mainieri and Roy Ayers. His solo on the 1985 live version of Sting's 'I Burn For You' is regarded as one of the best examples of recorded drum soloing. Hakim has also performed and recorded with many other artists including Madonna, Mariah Carey, Jewel, Celine Dion, Lee Ritenour, Toninho Horta and David Sanborn. He also collaborated with George Benson on the latter's 1983 release *In Your Eyes*, contributing his composition 'Being With You'. In the mid 1980s Omar Hakim recorded on David Bowie's most successful album *Let's Dance* and the multi-million selling *Brothers In Arms* by Dire Straits, allegedly cutting his parts in two days. Of late he recorded 'Get Lucky' by Daft Punk. Omar Hakim is also a multi-instrumentalist, a composer and an expert programmer. The fluidity of his technique is legendary. He is amongst a select group of instrumentalists whose work has been in constant demand for the last four decades.

Techno

John Scofield
Words & Music by John Scofield

[11]
[13]
[15]
cont. sim.
[17]
[19]
[21]
[23]
[25]

[27]
[29]
1.
2.
R L L R R R L R L
[32]
B
[34]
f
cont. sim.
[36]
[38]
R L L R R L R L R L
6
[40]
C
[42]
mf

cont. sim.
[44]
[46]
[48]
Drums solo over hits with increasing intensity
[50]
2
[52]
2
[54]
1. 2.
2
[56]
3.
[58]
f

Walkthrough

'Techno' appeared on John Scofield's *Still Warm* album and featured Omar Hakim on drums. The drum part is based around a classic hand-to-hand 16th-note hi-hat pattern but with a syncopated twist. Essentially it's a two-measure pattern which misses out the backbeat on beat 2 in every second measure. Instead the snare at this point is replaced by the bass drum which plays a variety of 16th-note based figures.

Intro (Measures 1–9)

Measures 1–2

The piece begins with a two-beat fill played on the snare before heading into the main groove. This two-measure pattern essentially sets the scene for most of the track. Notice how the first measure is a straightforward enough 16th-note based groove but also how the left hand begins a series of three upbeat 16th-note accents on the last 16th-note of measure 1, with the first note being an open sound. In order for this open note to be of the correct 16th-note duration, the left foot must close the hi-hats on the downbeat of the following measure.

You'll also notice that the backbeat that would be expected on beat 2 of the second measure is missing, and is instead replaced by the bass drum. Although the figure played here sets the scene for the rest of the intro and A section, it doesn't remain static, and the bass drum moves through a variety of figures.

Measures 3 and 5

Occasionally the hi-hats are opened for the duration of a quarter-note on beat 1 of the second measure, as in measures 3 and 5. Also watch out for the five-stroke roll on the '&' of beat 2 in measure 5.

A Section (Measures 9–33)

The A section is 24 measures long and repeated twice. The first eight measures are notated specifically, but from this point you're free to experiment and develop your own ideas based upon those played so far.

Measure 10

Notice how measure 10 has no backbeat at all, with the snare on beat 4 replaced by upbeat accents on the hi-hats.

Measure 33

In the second time measure at measure 33, in order to comfortably play the upbeat 16th-note figure down the toms and through beat 3, the sticking will need to switch into the right hand using the double left on beat 2.

B Section (Measures 34–41)

At letter B we head over to the ride cymbal where the bass drum and snare play a more traditional pattern. Notice also the rise in dynamics to forte. However the most interesting part is the movement between the bell of the ride cymbal and stepped left foot which are essentially alternating eighth-notes, with the ride bell on the quarter-note and the left foot playing the upbeat eighth-note. Letter B is eight measures long and ends with fill based around a six-stroke roll moving from high tom to snare.

C Section (Measures 42–59)

Letter C is essentially the same drum groove as letter A and lasts for eight measures. Notice the drop in dynamics back to mezzo forte.

Measure 50

In measure 50 we reach the drum solo. This is 24 measures long and played over a syncopated two-measure vamp laid down by the band. The challenge here is to retain your place, counting measures and/or numbers of repeats if necessary. Notice also the instruction to increase intensity as the solo progresses, with the dynamics rising to forte for the final two measures. In situations such as this it can be effective to allow time for the solo to develop, perhaps avoiding immediately playing 'loud and fast' which can sometimes be a reflex when allowed the space to solo. Instead perhaps try exploring the space, develop ideas and try using the rhythm within the vamp itself as inspiration for your own ideas.

SONG TITLE: RAZORHEAD
GENRE: METAL
TEMPO: 168 BPM

TECH FEATURES: GHOSTING
BROKEN 16TH ROLLS
ODD TIME SIGNATURES

COMPOSER: JASON BOWLD

PERSONNEL: JASON BOWLD (ALL PARTS)

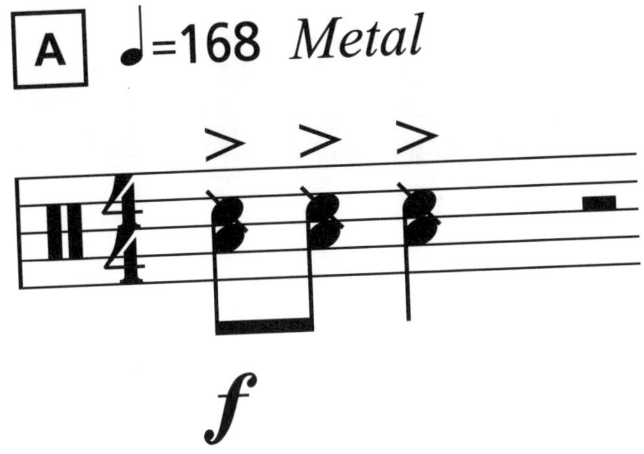

OVERVIEW

'Razorhead' is influenced by Slipknot, Sepultura and Bullet For My Valentine. You will find relentless, regular changes in rhythm and note values as well as dynamic subtleties and odd time signatures here.

STYLE FOCUS

Good technique and stamina are required to play metal convincingly. More importantly, an even consistency should be achieved with the volume of backbeats on the snare and the bass drum beats. This consistency should be continued into any drum fills so that the intensity level demanded by the style doesn't drop. Also, try to balance or mix yourself when playing metal because you may find that you tend to overhit the cymbals and hi-hats.

THE BIGGER PICTURE

The British band Black Sabbath are recognised as the creators of metal. Their self-titled debut was released in 1970, and soon after bands such as Judas Priest and Iron Maiden became part of the New Wave Of British Heavy Metal that influenced the faster sub-genres of thrash and speed metal in the 1980s.

Metallica, Anthrax, Slayer and Megadeth (also known as The Big Four) are the most famous of the bands that emerged from the 1980s thrash scene. The use of two bass drums became common practice among drummers Dave Lombardo (Slayer), Charlie Benante (Anthrax) and Lars Ulrich (Metallica), who were reaching speeds of 200 bpm.

In the 1990s nu metal bands Korn and Limp Bizkit mixed styles such as death metal and rap, while Slipknot continued to push the boundaries of speed thanks to their drummer Joey Jordison.

Since the turn of the millennium, the rise of groups like Lamb Of God, Mastodon and Trivium led to the New Wave Of American Heavy Metal, while the British group Bullet For My Valentine reached number 3 in the US Billboard charts in 2010 with their album *Fever*.

RECOMMENDED LISTENING

Jordison's drumming on *Iowa* (2001) by Slipknot is a great starter, as is Lombardo's work on Slayer's *Reign In Blood* (1986). For vintage drumming try Bill Ward on *Black Sabbath* and *Paranoid* (both 1970). For a modern approach, Ulrich's playing on *Master Of Puppets* (1986) features some excellent compositions.

Razorhead

Jason Bowld

[31]
[35]
D.𝄋. al Coda 𝄌
[39]
𝄌 Coda
[43]
mf
[47]
[50]
f
[53]
cont. sim.
Fill
[57]
Fill
Fill

[61]
ff
D
Choke
[65]
Choke
[69]
[73]
[77]
1.
[81]
2.
Fill
[84]
E
[87]
f

[91]
[95]
[99]
[102]
[105]
F
[109]
ff
[113]
Fill
[117]
3

Walkthrough

A Section (Measures 1–16)

The intro is based on stabs which the drums solo around. This leads to the groove that locks in with the guitar riff.

Measures 1–8 | *Stab solo*
Try to emphasise the stabs throughout. They are counted as "1&2" and can be disguised within drum fills for added flow.

Measures 11–16 | *Groove fills*
In measure 12, the most comfortable sticking would be to use your left hand for the snare and travel around the crashes and toms with your right. Measure 16 concludes with a quarter-note triplet fill. Count "1-trip-let 3-tripl-let" to keep your timing accurate.

B Section (Measures 17–26)

This section can be interpreted as the verse of the song and features a heavy tom groove that accentuates the guitar riff.

Measures 17–25 | *Tom groove*
This groove is intense on the right hand so try not to choke the sticks, as this will inhibit your speed.

Measure 26 | *Snare roll*
The key features of this roll are the offbeat accents before the beat. A loose grip is vital for power and consistency.

C Section (Measures 27–42)

This section features the chorus of the song and returns to the intro guitar riff but with a half-time feel.

Measures 27–34 | *Chorus groove*
The feel of this two-measure groove is a mixture of normal and half-time. Focus on the crashes on beat 1 and beat 3 of each respective measure because these match the harmonic shifts in the music.

Measures 35–40 | *Half-time groove*
Watch out for the displaced backbeat onto beat 4 in the second measure of this two-measure groove.

Coda (Measures 43–64)

The *Coda* has a medium loud groove that increases dynamically towards the choruses.

Measures 43–52 | *Layered ghost groove*
After the *Coda*s initial fill, you will play a groove in measure 45 which features a sticking that is similar to an inverted paradiddle: R L L R L R R L. The only difference is that the last right features a layered left double. There is a more fragmented approach and an open hi-hat on beat 3 of the second measure. The pre-chorus snare roll returns in measure 52, where the dynamics increase to loud (Fig. 1).

Measures 53–64 | *Extended chorus groove*
Towards the end of this extended chorus, a two-measure groove develops that must be played loud with snare and crashes on every dotted quarter note. The bass drum fills the gaps, so you will have to be careful not to rush your hands.

D Section (Measures 65–86)

This section features the three stabs that characterise the main riff of the whole song. These occur at the start of every other measure with the drums changing every eight measures, so use this as a compass to find your groove.

E Section (Measures 87–108)

This section starts with a drop in dynamics with a half-time groove that progresses to the 5/4 section.

Measures 103–105 | *5/4 groove*
Try counting "1&2 3&4 5&" as a way of tackling this groove's odd timing (Fig. 2).

F Section (Measures 109–119)

Make sure you observe that the final chorus should be played louder and faster than the others.

Fig. 1: Layered ghost groove

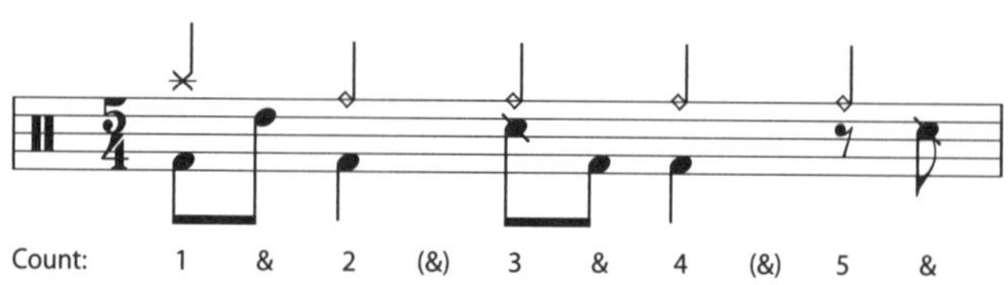

Fig. 2: 5/4 groove

Buena Havana

SONG TITLE: BUENA HAVANA
GENRE: SALSA
TEMPO: 204 BPM

TECH FEATURES: GHOST NOTES
POLYRHYTHMS

COMPOSER: NOAM LEDERMAN

PERSONNEL: STUART RYAN (GTR)
HENRY THOMAS (BASS)
NOAM LEDERMAN (DRUMS)
KISHON KHAN (PIANO)
FERGUS GERRAND (PERC)
RICHARD PARDY (SAX)
STEVE WALKER (TRUMPET)

OVERVIEW

A Cuban flavour runs through 'Buena Havana', bringing with it the spirit of the Buena Vista Social Club and bandleaders Tito Puente and Johnny Pacheco. It features polyrhythms, the clave rhythm, and ghost notes among its techniques.

STYLE FOCUS

The clave rhythm is an integral ingredient of salsa, mambo and Latin jazz and instantly separates these styles from North American music. The clave is usually played by a percussionist using the sticks that give the pattern its name but the drummer can often follow the clave somewhere on his kit: on the ride cymbal, a cowbell, or using a cross-stick on the snare. The music doesn't always feature the bass drum played on the '1', which gives it a very different feel from rock, swing or R&B.

THE BIGGER PICTURE

The great trumpeter Dizzy Gillespie brought Latin rhythms to American and European audiences by incorporating Afro Cuban beats into his music, particularly on the song 'Manteca' (a hit in 1947).

In the 1950s, mambo enjoyed a surge of popularity in America thanks to musicians like Tito Puente, a bandleader who combined showmanship and musical excellence to sustain a lengthy career. On the American TV show *I Love Lucy*, Desi Arnaz played the titular Lucy's husband and happened to lead a Cuban orchestra, and so brought Latin music into America's living rooms.

In the 1960s, Pacheco kept the Afro Cuban rhythms flowing and launched a short-lived dance craze called the Pachanga.

In 1999, the long-running Cuban ensemble The Buena Vista Social Club suddenly found itself in the spotlight thanks to a documentary about the group, *Mandinga*, proving that the music's appeal is timeless.

RECOMMENDED LISTENING

Puente's album *Dance Mania* was a hit in 1958 when mambo fever swept America. 'El Cayuco' is a great example of the clave in a Latin jazz context. La Excelencia write modern salsa and 'La Lucha' and 'American Sueno' are worth hearing. For Afro Cuban polyrhythms in a fusion context, try *Jungle City* (2009) by Alex Acuña and his trio. Finally, hear the veterans The Buena Vista Social Club on 'Mandinga'.

Buena Havana

Noam Lederman

[24]
1.
2.
Fill
[27]
D
Develop on repeat
[31]
[34]
[37]
E
[39]
mp

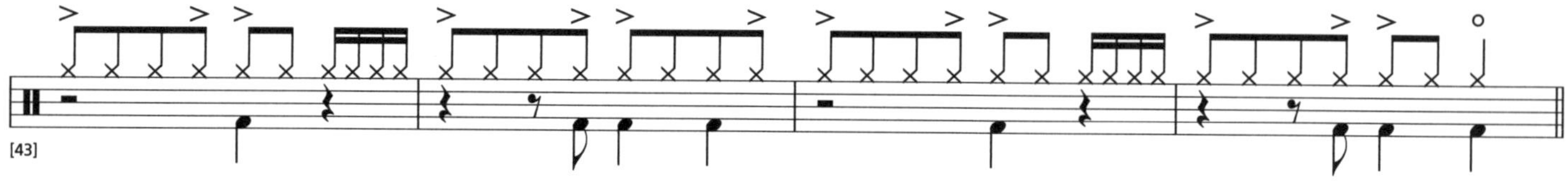

Drum Solo (16 measures)

Solo around stabs

Trumpet Solo (32 measures)

† Cross stick and rim of floor tom

[64]
[68]
Fill
Develop on repeat
f
[72]
[76]
Develop
[80]
1.
2.
[84]

Walkthrough

A Section (Measures 1–4)

After the initial two-measures rest, there are notated stabs and a fill that prepares for the entry of the groove in measure 5. The count-in is based on half notes. This is common in fast Latin pieces because having the full four beats can be off-putting.

B Section (Measures 5–20)

The 2:3 clave salsa groove enters in measure 5 and the hi-hat foot is added on beats 1 and 3 from measure 13.

Measures 5–6 | *Salsa*

The cross stick pattern in this salsa beat plays the clave, the foundation of many Latin beats. The clave in this groove features two strokes in the first measure and three in the second, and is, therefore, referred to as a 2:3 clave. Practise the clave with a metronome to ensure fluency and a consistent pulse. The next step is adding the ride cymbal pattern which plays the lead rhythmic phrase. This is most commonly played on the ride cymbal, bell, cowbell and rims and referred to as 'cascara' in Latin music. Co-ordinating the clave and cascara with perfect unison is your goal. Slowing the tempo down and counting beats will help you to understand the rhythmic phrases. The final step is adding the bass drum pattern on the fourth beat and the offbeat of the second (Fig. 1).

C Section (Measures 21–30)

The cascara changes and moves to the bell of ride, while there are clave variations with the cross stick and toms.

Measures 21–30 | *Balance and sound in Latin*

Traditionally, there were no drum kit players in Latin music. Even today most salsa bands will have two to three percussionists but no kit player. Therefore, your approach to Latin drumming and especially its sound production is critical. In most Latin grooves each drum voice is supposed to imitate a traditional percussion instrument. It is important that you understand what sound you are trying to achieve before playing this on the kit. The balance between kit parts is dependent on the specific style. In salsa the cascara and clave will be more prominent, while in songo the balance should be more even because it is a linear beat.

D Section (Measures 31–38)

The songo groove is introduced in this section. The dynamic levels of the snare and open hi-hat are vital to this groove.

Measures 31–38 | *Songo*

Although the hi-hat varies between open and closed, it is consistent enough for you to use as an anchor. Co-ordinate the bass drum pattern with the hi-hat then move to the snare. Initially, play all the snares at a similar dynamic level until the rhythms are correct and your four limbs are working in perfect unison. Next, focus on the accented and ghost snares and ensure that the dynamic changes do not affect the flow of time (Fig. 2).

E Section (Measures 39–46)

In this section the focus is on the hi-hat pattern. The combination of accented strokes and fast 16th notes will require solid technique.

Measures 39–46 | *Doubles vs singles*

The 16th notes on the hi-hat can be played with singles or doubles. In both techniques, it is recommended that you use your fingers to manipulate the stick and achieve balanced strokes. Playing these types of 16th notes with doubles will be useful in many styles. The five stroke roll rudiment is an especially handy technique to have in your arsenal.

F Section (Measures 47–55)

This is the drum solo. You will need to pay attention to the notated stabs.

G Section (Measures 56–88)

The section opens with a 3:2 clave groove with the cascara played on the rim of the floor tom. From measure 72 the groove is similar to the one that was introduced in section C but with some variations.

Fig. 1: Salsa

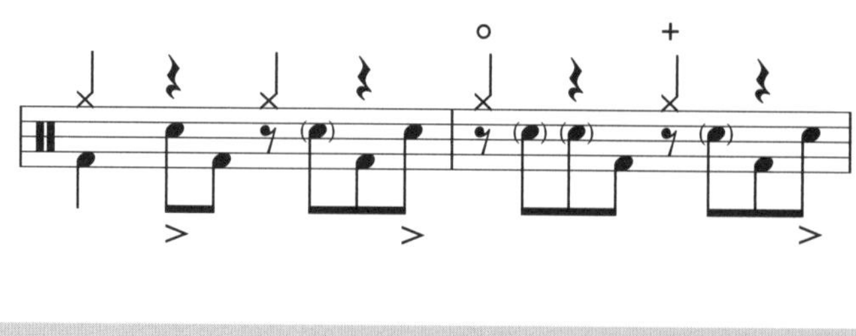

Fig. 2: Songo

SONG TITLE: THE BEAN
GENRE: PROG ROCK
TEMPO: 192 BPM (EIGHTH NOTES)

TECH FEATURES: ODD TIME SIGNATURES
32ND NOTE ROLLS
SYNCOPATION

COMPOSER: PETER HUNTINGTON

PERSONNEL: CHARLIE GRIFFITHS (GUITAR/BASS)
NOAM LEDERMAN (DRUMS)

OVERVIEW

'The Bean' is a prog rock track inspired by the band Rush and the phenomenal drumming of Neil Peart. The track features many different odd time signatures as well as a variety of fills of differing note values ranging from 16ths to 32nds.

STYLE FOCUS

Prog rock relies heavily on the drummer to have a wide vocabulary of styles and skill sets. It is important to have a knowledge of world music styles like Latin and African as well as the usual knowledge of rock, funk and jazz. The prog rock drummer must be well-equipped to play polyrhythms, ostinatos, and have the ability to play at a wide range of dynamics because the music is diverse and can change its feel within the blink of an eye. A wide knowledge of styles is key when it comes to prog rock drumming.

THE BIGGER PICTURE

Progressive rock is a style of music that developed in the late 1960s and early 1970s when bands including King Crimson, Genesis, Pink Floyd and Rush rose to prominence with their eclectic sound of varying styles, complex arrangements and imaginative lyrical content.

Prog rock bands are known for their exceptional musical proficiency, especially their drummers. Neil Peart, drummer of Canadian trio Rush, is widely revered as one of the best drummers in the world having consistently won readers' polls in *Modern Drummer* magazine. Peart's style was heavily rooted in rock until the mid 1990s when he worked under the tutelage of jazz drummer Freddy Gruber. His drum solos are a highlight of Rush concerts and feature endless polyrhythms and snare drum solos, all of which take place on a rotating drum riser that has a traditional acoustic kit at the front and an electronic kit at the rear.

RECOMMENDED LISTENING

Rush have released over 17 albums in their career so far and it's worth checking out all of them. Their self-titled debut (1974) features the group's first drummer John Rutsey and provides an interesting comparison to their later albums. The 1985 release *Power Windows* and the recent *Clockwork Angels* (2012) are also notable records. The tracks 'Limelight', 'The Body Electric' and 'The Main Monkey Business' all highlight Peart's exciting style.

The Bean

Peter Huntington

E
[33]
Fill
[36]
Fill
[39]
D.C. al Coda
Coda
[41]
[45]
Develop
[49]
[53]
[57]

Walkthrough

A Section (Measures 1–4)

The A section features rhythmic stabs in 5/8 with technical and dynamic drum fills.

Measure 1 | *5/8*
The time signature indicates that there are five eighth notes in each measure. The stabs in measures 1 and 3 are placed on the first and fourth eighth notes as well as between the second and third. Try using a count of "1 2& 3 4 5" in order to understand the stabs. Listen to the track too, because the guitar and bass play the same riff (Fig. 1).

Measure 2 | *Singles*
This type of fill is typical of progressive rock and requires solid singles technique. In order to play these fast 32nd notes accurately, it is recommended that you use a combination of wrist and fingers technique. Loosening the grip at the right moment will allow your fingers to manipulate the drumstick and perform the fast strokes with minimal effort. However, your wrist will give the strokes more weight and assist in achieving a balanced sound.

B Section (Measures 5–20)

In this section the time signature changes to 6/8 (i.e. six eighth notes per measure). The full groove begins in measure 13 and there are gentle stabs in the previous eight measures.

Measures 13–20 | *6/8 groove*
The consistent eighth note hi-hats can be your anchor in this groove. Focus on the snare and bass drum pattern and aim to perform the rim-shot snares with conviction. The backbeat snares are played between the eighth note hi-hats; therefore, you might feel a natural tendency to rush. In this case breaking the groove down into measures (even beats, if necessary) and practising at a slower tempo is the only way of ensuring that it is played correctly.

C Section (Measures 21–24)

This is a reprise of the introduction with different drum fills.

Measure 22 | *Linear fill*
This fill includes ten 16th notes played between the snare, hi-hat and bass drum. Playing 16th-note phrases between three voices creates a rhythmic illusion and when done well can be impressive. Because the fill follows the linear concept, you can not use any part of the kit as an anchor and will have to rely on the backing track and your own sense of pulse.

D Section (Measures 25–32)

The 16 measures of the guitar solo section consist of one main 7/8 groove with straightforward 16th-note fills.

Measures 25–32 | *7/8 groove*
Initially, practise the 7/8 groove in measure 25 until you feel comfortable with this time signature. You can use a metronome, but working with a drum machine or loops that include more instruments will make this more enjoyable and realistic. The key to the groove is the 16th-note snare towards the end of the measure. Focus on this snare and ensure that the flow on the hi-hats is not affected. The written fills are not technically challenging but coming out of them with seamless synchronisation can be tricky (Fig. 2).

E Section (Measures 33–59)

The 7/8 groove develops on the ride cymbal with eighth notes on your hi-hat foot and occasional bell of ride. You have the opportunity to play your own improvised fills. Listen to prog drummers, and Neil Peart in particular, for ideas on improvising in this style. Remember that when repeating sections A and B (on ***D.C.***) you need to develop the part according to your interpretation of the style.

Measures 41–42 | *6/8 half time groove*
In the ***Coda*** section, the 6/8 groove changes to half time feel, where there is only one rim-shot snare per measure. In order to fill the gaps and ensure that the groove continues to flow, there are ghost notes on the snare to perform. Position your left hand in the place that allows you to perform the rim-shot and ghost notes comfortably and, if needed, change the height and angle of the snare.

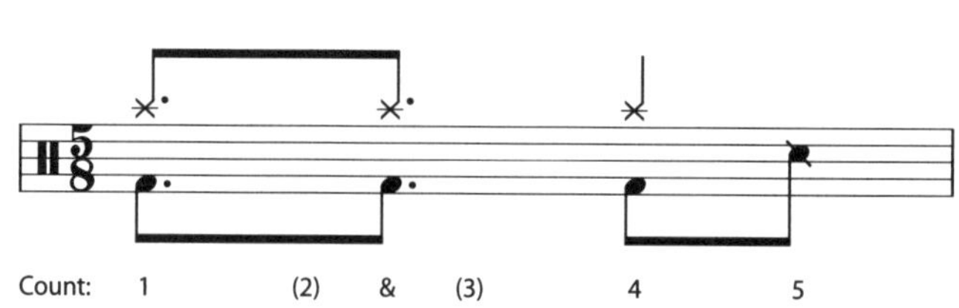

Fig. 1: 5/8

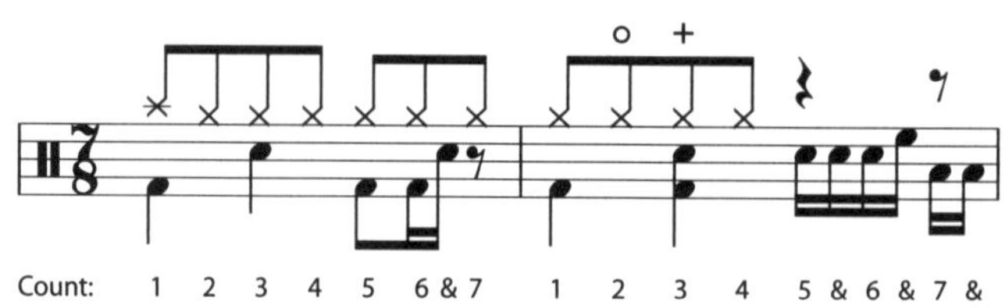

Fig. 2: 7/8 groove

Eastern Adventure

SONG TITLE: EASTERN ADVENTURE
GENRE: DRUM AND BASS
TEMPO: 166 BPM

TECH FEATURES: 'AMEN BREAK'
FAST 16TH-NOTE PHRASES
STYLISTIC SOLO/
DEVELOPMENT

COMPOSER: NEEL DHORAJIWALA

PERSONNEL: NOAM LEDERMAN (DRUMS)
NEEL D (PROD)
CAMILLO TIRADO (TABLA)

OVERVIEW

'Eastern Adventure' is a drum and bass track written with influences from the world music scene.

STYLE FOCUS

Early drum and bass productions relied upon sped-up drum breaks sampled from funk records. These syncopated grooves give drum and bass its unique sound as opposed to the straight four-to-the-floor feel of house, techno and trance. Because these breaks were sampled, the drum parts were rarely performed live. However, since the late 1990s drummers have been emulating these grooves live on drum kits. The acclaimed Jojo Mayer is arguably the greatest live performer of traditional drum and bass grooves.

THE BIGGER PICTURE

Drum and bass stemmed from the British rave scene of the late 1980s. Its signature sound was a combination of sped-up breakbeats and sub-bass lines. From the beginning the Jamaican dub reggae and ragga styles were an influence, although this sound was later to develop into a distinct sub genre of its own called jungle. The differences between jungle and drum and bass are much debated but, as a generalisation, jungle came to refer to the original sound of chopped sampled breaks and reggae vocals, whereas drum and bass was a term applied to the music as it grew towards more programmed grooves.

From the late 1990s, drum and bass stars Goldie, Roni Size / Reprazent and Nitin Sawhney embraced live musicianship and performed with acoustic/electric drum kit hybrids, synths and samplers.

RECOMMENDED LISTENING

Goldie's 1995 debut, *Timeless,* was a crossover hit that changed the course of drum and bass with live female vocals and instrumentation. 1997's Mercury Prize winning *New Forms* by Roni Size/Reprazent also featured live instruments while retaining jungle's rough urban edge. From the more world influenced side of drum and bass, notable tracks include Nitin Sawhney's 'Nadia' and 'Breathing Light'.

In its early days, drum and bass sold mainly on 12" vinyl as singles, so explore the output of record labels of that time, many of which were run by DJs and producers. Goldie's Metalheadz, Andy C's Ram Records, LTJ Bukem's Good Looking Records and DJ Friction's Shogun Audio are all great reference points.

Eastern Adventure

Neel Dhorajiwala

[25]
To Coda
Fill
[29]
C
[33]
f
[37]
3
f mf mp
[41]
f
[45]

D **Drum Solo** (8 measures as written, 8 measures improvised)

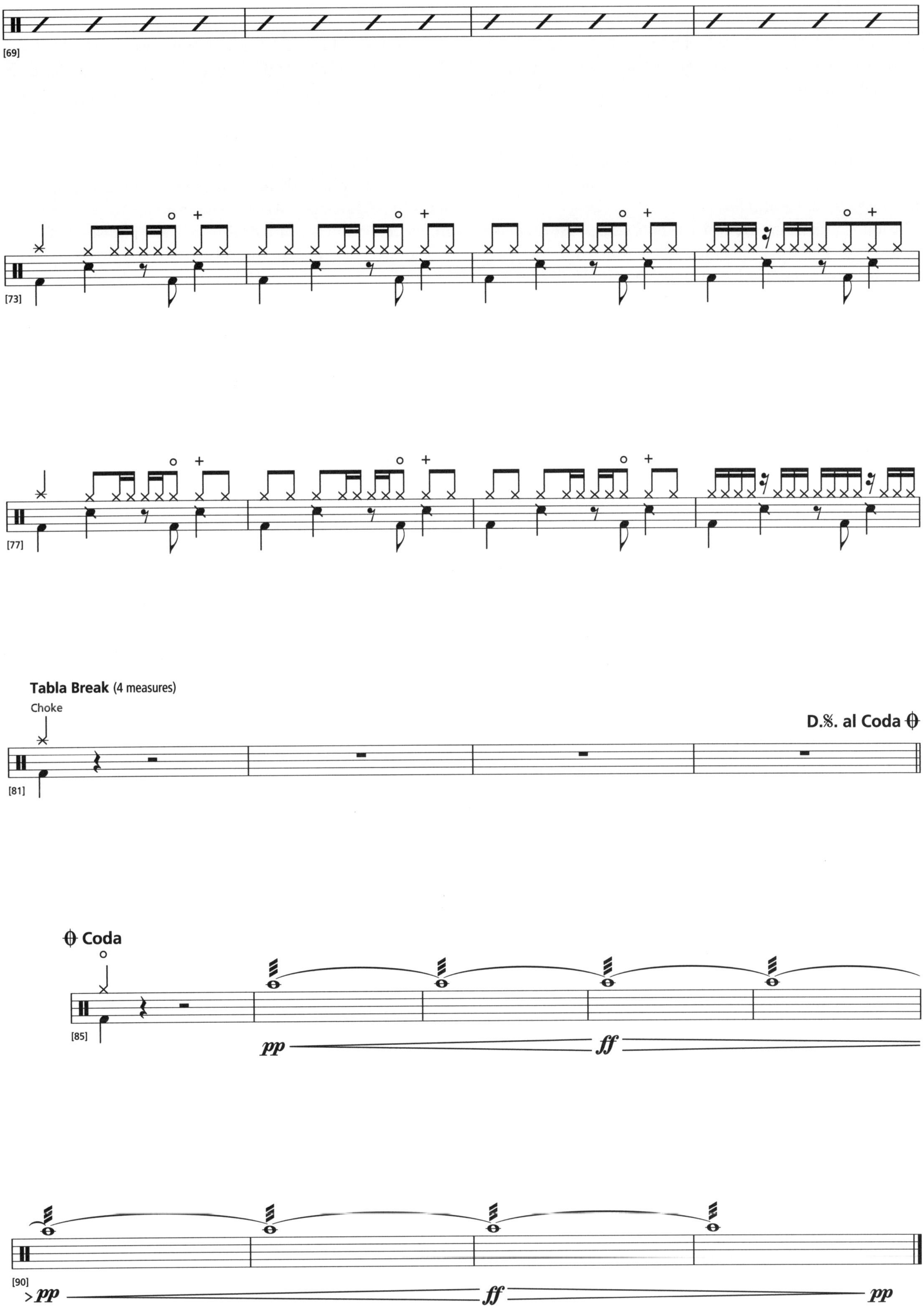
[69]
[73]
[77]
Tabla Break (4 measures)
Choke
D.%. al Coda
[81]
Coda
[85]
pp
ff
[90]
pp
ff
pp

Walkthrough

A Section (Measures 1–16)

This section features the main groove of the piece. In the first eight measures it is led by quarter notes on the bell and, from measure 9, eighth notes on the ride cymbal. In measure 9 the ghost note pattern on the snare becomes more intense. The section ends with a crash hit with no bass drum.

Measures 9–12 | *'Amen break'*

The four-measure groove which is notated in these measures is also known as the 'Amen break'. This groove was sampled from the funky soul track 'Amen, Brother' by The Winstons by dance music producers in the late 1980s. It was especially popular among drum and bass and jungle producers. The key to this groove is the ghost notes and one displaced snare at the end of the third measure. Ensure that the eighth notes on the ride cymbal are even and consistent throughout the beat.

B Section (Measures 17–32)

The dynamic level changes in section B and the groove moves to the hi-hat and cross stick snare. The variations of the cross stick and open/closed hi-hats will drive the beat forward, so pay attention to the pulse of the backing track.

C Section (Measures 33–48)

In this section the groove returns to the ride and becomes heavier with rim-shot snares. There is a fill in measure 40 that requires highly reliable dynamic control.

Measures 33–48 | *Reverse engineering*

This term has been used by drummers to describe the action of translating and playing programmed jungle and drum and bass beats on the acoustic drum kit. The primary techniques that will be used in this process are: the Moeller method, push-pull and heel-toe bass drum. These techniques are thoroughly explained and demonstrated in Steve Smith's educational DVD *Drumset Technique*. Sound production is also an important part of reverse engineering. In drum and bass it is vital that every drum voice is played as evenly and consistently as possible.

D Section (Measures 49–64)

This is the drum solo section where you have the opportunity to demonstrate your understanding of the style. After playing the first eight measures as notated, improvise and show your technical ability and musicality.

Measures 49–64 | *Drum solo*

Listening to drum and bass music will give you ideas of the type of programmed drum loops and fills used in this style. Try to imitate and recreate these using the drum kit, focusing on sound production and feel. The drummer Jojo Mayer explains in his DVD *Secret Weapons For The Modern Drummer* the origins of the 'Amen break' and shows his own ways of developing electronic beats around the acoustic kit.

E Section (Measures 65–94)

This section starts with an intense crash cymbal beat that needs to be developed stylistically. From measure 73 the groove returns to the hi-hat with 16th-note phrases that lead to the tabla break in measure 81. Remember that when repeating section B (after ***D.S.***) you need to develop the part according to your interpretation. The dynamic changes during the cymbal rolls in the ***Coda*** are an important part of this piece.

Measures 73–76 | *Sixteenth note phrases*

Playing 16th-notes at the speed of 166 bpm requires practice and planning. The four 16th-notes in measures 73–75 can be played with alternate sticking starting with your right hand. The longer phrases can be played with similar sticking but many drummers who specialise in this style recommend using paradiddle sticking. This will lead to a more consistent sound from the backbeat since your left hand will play both backbeats in the measure (Fig. 1).

Measures 86–93 | *Cymbal rolls*

The three lines below the cymbal note indicate that a roll should be played on the crash in these measures. This is usually played with single strokes, but can also be played with doubles. Aim to achieve a fluent and consistent sound from the crash and pay attention to the dynamic changes (Fig. 2).

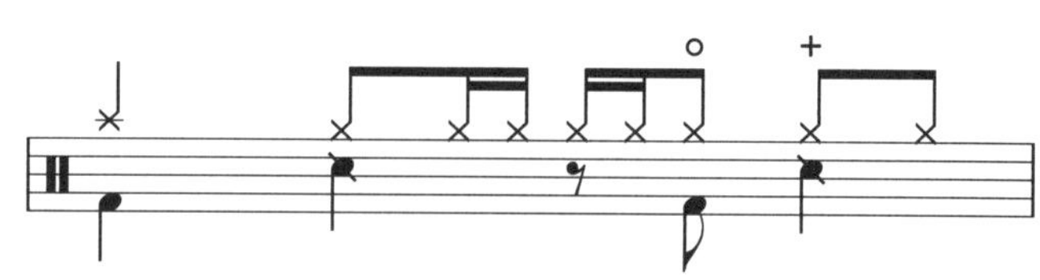

Fig. 1: Sixteenth note phrases

Fig. 2: Cymbal rolls

Full English Breckerfest

SONG TITLE: FULL ENGLISH BRECKERFEST
GENRE: FUNK
TEMPO: 115 BPM

TECH FEATURES: SYNCOPATED STABS
SNARE RIM-SHOTS
CHANGING TIME SIGNATURES

COMPOSER: LUKE ALDRIDGE

PERSONNEL: STUART RYAN (GTR)
HENRY THOMAS (BASS)
NOAM LEDERMAN (DRUMS)
ROSS STANLEY (KEYS)
RICHARD PARDY (SAX)
STEVE WALKER (TRUMPET)

OVERVIEW

'Full English Breckerfest' is a funk track incorporating elements of jazz and fusion in the style of bands like The Brecker Brothers and Herbie Hancock. It features syncopated stabs, snare rim-shots and changing time signatures among its techniques.

STYLE FOCUS

In a jazz or fusion influenced funk style the melodic and harmonic elements tend to be more developed than perhaps a standard funk tune, but ultimately rhythm still plays the most important part. This track's main keyboard riff uses a 16th-note push at the end of the measure tied over to the first beat of the next measure. This is reflected in the other rhythm section parts including the drums.

THE BIGGER PICTURE

Miles Davis and Herbie Hancock were both established figures on the jazz scene when James Brown created funk in the late 1960s. Both men were seduced by funk's earthiness and wondered how their own improvised music might sound with a stable harmonic base, and with the complex chords and quick changes of be bop discarded completely. Davis' *Bitches Brew* (1970) and Hancock's *Headhunters* (1973) provided the answer and inspired a generation of jazz funk groups.

Bands that followed included the Mahavishnu Orchestra, with the great Billy Cobham on drums, and The Brecker Brothers. Michael (tenor saxophone) and Randy Brecker (trumpet) were top session players but also recorded and toured with their own band playing original material during the 1970s. They reformed with a new rhythm section, including Dennis Chambers on drums, for the 1992 album *Return Of The Brecker Brothers*.

RECOMMENDED LISTENING

'Chameleon' from *Headhunters* is a jazz funk standard with Harvey Mason on drums. Other great Hancock albums include the follow-up *Thrust* (1974) and live album *Flood* (1975) with Mike Clarke, both of which have a unique feel with such a different player behind the kit. The Brecker Brothers' tracks 'Rocks', 'Skunk Funk' and 'Sponge' are the funkiest of their 1970s recordings and feature a number of drum legends from Steve Jordan to Terry Bozzio. 'Outta Here' and 'Rage' by Lettuce feature the amazing Adam Deitch on drums.

Full English Breckerfest

Luke Aldridge

[15]
C
[17]
[19]
[21]
[23]
D
[25]
[27]
[29]

[31]
Trumpet Solo (8 measures)
E
Develop
[33]
[35]
[38]
Saxophone Solo (12 measures)
F
[41]
[43]
[45]
[47]

[49]
[51]
G
[53]
Develop
[55]
[58]
H
[61]
Develop (around stabs)
[63]
[66]

Walkthrough

A Section (Measures 1–8)
The intro features a four measure build-up consisting of 16th-note hi-hats and the main funk groove which enters in measure 5.

Measure 1 | *Accenting the hi-hat*
Playing accented strokes requires solid hands technique and preparation. The most common way of sticking this pattern is alternate starting with the right hand. Remember that lifting your hand higher and hitting the hi-hat with the neck part of your stick will naturally create an accented sound.

Measure 2 | *Doubles vs singles*
The 32nd notes on the hi-hat can be played with singles or doubles. With either it is recommended that you use your fingers to manipulate the stick and achieve balanced strokes. Playing these types of 32nd notes with doubles will be useful in many styles. The five stroke roll rudiment is an especially handy technique to have in your arsenal (Fig. 1).

Measure 4 | *Sixteenth note push*
This rhythmic phrase will be repeated many times in the piece. It gives this groove a unique, funky, almost jumpy feel and must be played with good synchronisation to the backing track. The main challenge is pushing the last 16th note in a measure and not playing the '1' in the following measure. Hopefully, you have already developed an internal sense of pulse because this will be needed here.

B Section (Measures 9–16)
The funk groove that was introduced in measure 5 is continued in this section with added ghost notes on the snare.

C Section (Measures 17–24)
In this section the groove moves between the ride cymbal and hi-hat. The bass drum pattern is more intense and the bell of ride strokes in measure 23 emphasise the down beats.

Measure 20 | *Syncopated phrase*
The counting for this phrase is "3 e - a - e - a" and there are various sticking options that you can use. This phrase is an integral part of the piece, so make sure you are comfortable with it before attempting the whole track. Remember that when playing the 'e' and 'a' there will be a natural tendency to rush ahead of the click or track (Fig. 2).

D Section (Measures 25–32)
The groove remains on the ride cymbal with similar 16th-note pushes and occasional ghost notes of the snare.

E Section (Measures 33–40)
The trumpet solo features a breakdown type groove based on the hi-hat. The counting for this rhythmic phrase is "1 e & 2 e &". Listen to the backing track and develop the drum part according to your musicality and technical ability. The drumming of Dennis Chambers and Terry Bozzio will give you ideas for development in this style.

F Section (Measures 41–52)
The time signature changes from 7/8 to 4/4 every two measures with a musical bell pattern in measures 45-46 and 49–50. The stabs in measures 51–52 lead to the last two sections of the piece.

Measures 41–50 | *7/8 vs 4/4*
If you have access to any music software, program a simple track with a click that alternates between 7/8 and 4/4 every two measures. Play a simple beat and get comfortable with this change then slowly introduce elements from the written part and gradually build up the speed. Alternatively, count the beats throughout, use a metronome and develop a solid understanding of the pulse. Aim to achieve fluent changes with convincing funky drumming. The rhythmic displacement of the bell in the 7/8 measures will require advanced co-ordination and attention to sound production.

G & H sections (Measures 53–68)
Section G is a reprise of the B section but with space for you to develop the part. The groove is moved to the ride cymbal in section H and the written stabs need to be voiced around the kit according to your interpretation.

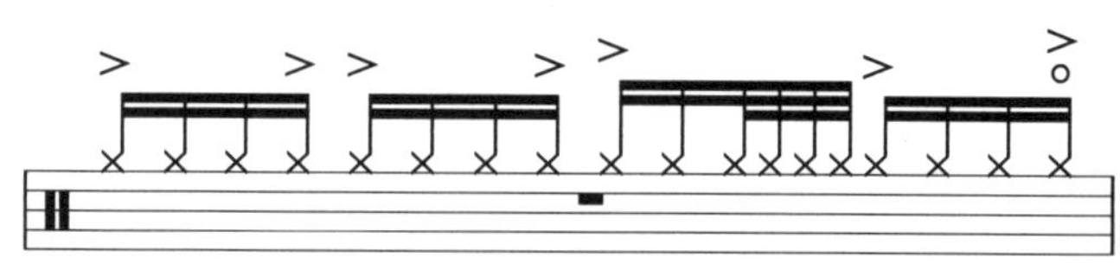

Fig. 1: Doubles vs singles

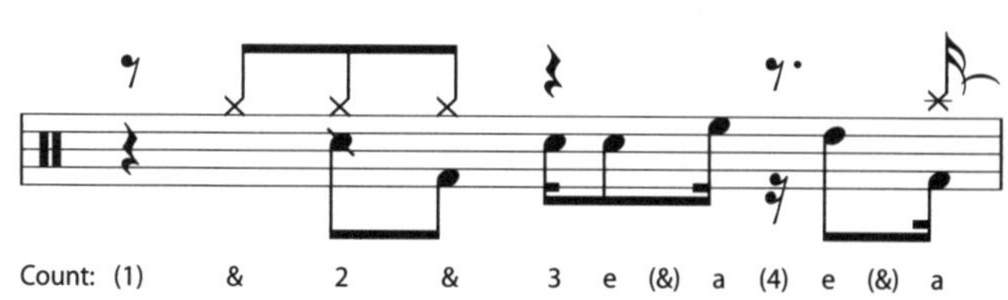

Fig. 2: Syncopated phrase

Kita's Five

SONG TITLE: KITA'S FIVE
GENRE: JAZZ
TEMPO: 172 BPM

TECH FEATURES: JAZZ SWING
ODD TIME SIGNATURES
ACCOMPANYING THE LEAD

COMPOSER: KITA STEUER

PERSONNEL: STUART RYAN (GTR)
HENRY THOMAS (BASS)
NOAM LEDERMAN (DRUMS)
ROSS STANLEY (KEYS)

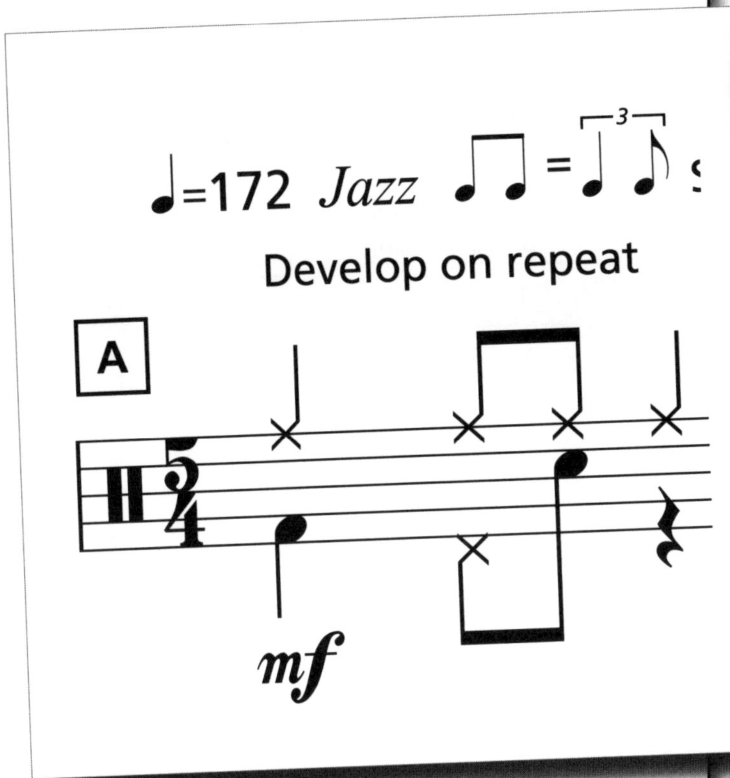

OVERVIEW

'Kita's Five' is written in the spirit of master jazz composer Dave Brubeck, who was a key figure in the cool jazz style, as well as musicians like pianist Vince Guaraldi, saxophonist Lester Young and trumpet player Chet Baker. This song features odd time signatures, swing and accompanying the lead among its various techniques.

STYLE FOCUS

'Kita's Five' is played in 5/4 time. You will notice that it is a swinging tune which calls for a rather light touch and dynamic control. Many drummers tackle odd time signatures by breaking them down into smaller units of two, three or four beats. When starting out, do not be scared by odd time signatures – play around with them and they will soon become comfortable. In jazz, your job is to be time-keeper and to accompany anyone taking a lead break so keep your ears open.

THE BIGGER PICTURE

Brubeck's style is considered part of cool jazz, which is less abrasive and aggressive than be bop. The Dave Brubeck Quartet's 1959 album, *Time Out,* began life as an attempt to explore different time signatures. Against the odds it became a hit, thanks in part to the brilliant single 'Take Five'. This track featured a standout solo by drummer Joe Morello, who was an influence on everyone from John Bonham (Led Zeppelin) to Max Weinberg (Bruce Springsteen's E Street Band). Morello, who died in 2011, was a technically dazzling player who cut more than 60 albums with Brubeck and is rightly remembered as one of the all-time greats.

RECOMMENDED LISTENING

Time Out is a must-have album for anyone who wishes to investigate the captivating sound of cool jazz, while the live album *At Carnegie Hall*, released in 1963 to widespread acclaim from peers and press, captures the legendary Dave Brubeck Quartet on top form. The Vince Guaraldi Trio recorded many beautiful tracks for the cartoon adaptations of Charles Schultz's Peanuts comic strip. Listen to their album *Jazz Impressions Of A Boy Named Charlie Brown* (1964) with Colin Bailey's clever drum parts on the bossa nova inspired 'Linus And Lucy', as well as the sweetly swinging 'Oh, Good Grief!'. *Chet Baker Sings*, from 1956, features a superb performance of 'My Funny Valentine' which is worth listening to.

Kita's Five

Kita Steuer

[22]
Straight 8's
C
[25]
[28]
Swung 8's
[31]
Guitar Solo (24 measures)
D
Develop
3
[34]
[37]
[40]

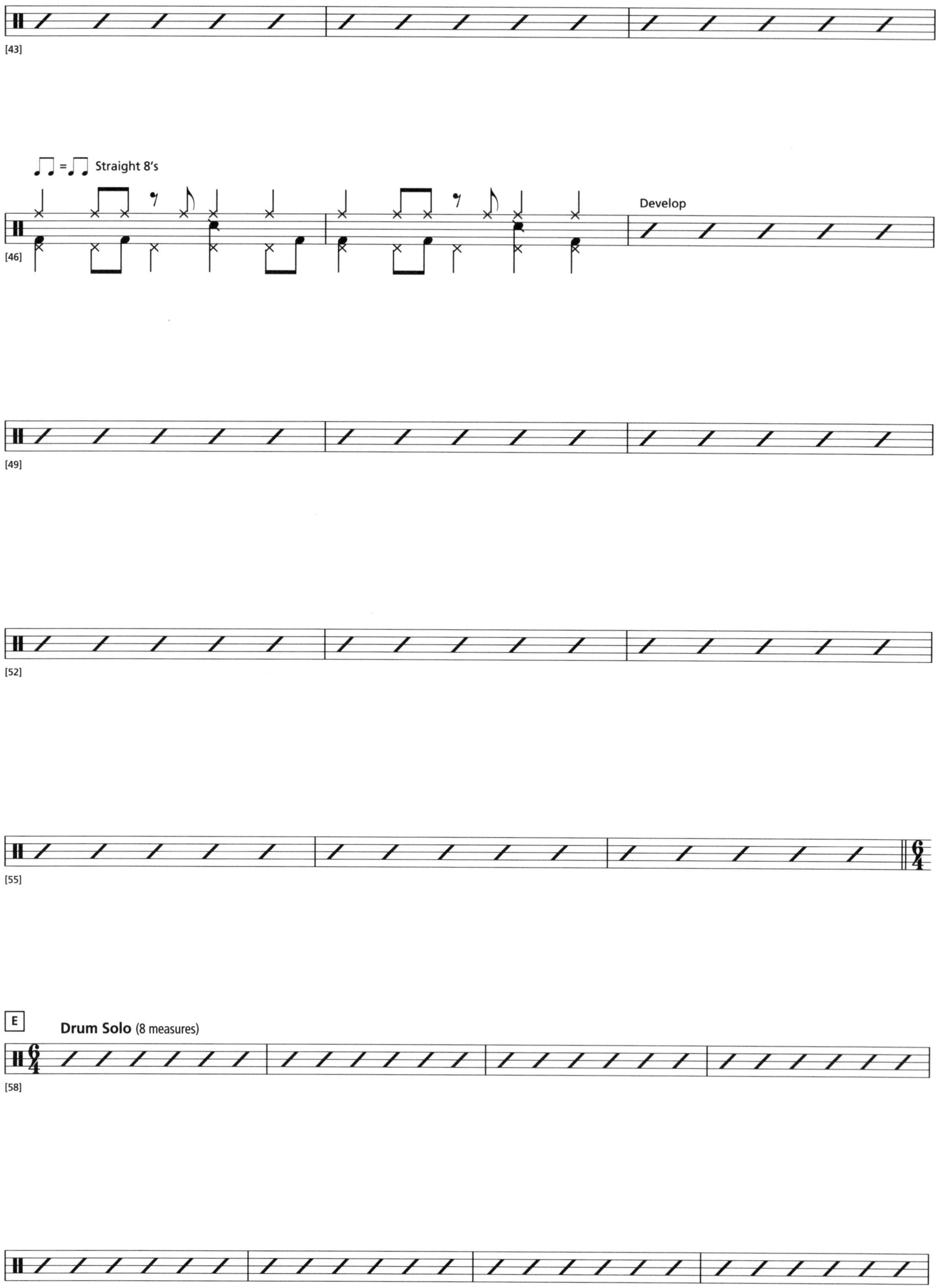
[43]
Straight 8's
Develop
[46]
[49]
[52]
[55]
E
Drum Solo (8 measures)
[58]
[62]

Straight 8's
F
[66]
[69]
Swung 8's
D.C. al Coda
[72]
Coda
Swung 8's
[75]
mf
[77]
stick on stick
p
[80]
Straight 8's
[83]
f
Straight 8's

Walkthrough

A Section (Measures 1–12)

In this section the swung 5/4 groove is introduced. It involves advanced four-way coordination and rhythmic stabs in measures 9 and 10.

Measure 1 | *5/4*

The time signature 5/4 indicates that there are five quarter notes in each measure. The ride pattern follows the rhythm "1 2& 3 4& 5" in most measures and the hi-hat foot is placed on beats 2 and 5. There is a bass drum on beat 1 and a varied snare pattern which is appropriate for the style. Practise the 5/4 jazz groove with a metronome or backing loop in order to secure the internal pulse.

Measure 1 | *Balance and sound in jazz*

In jazz drumming, the most common balance will be (from loudest to softest): ride cymbal, hi-hat foot, snare and bass drum. The ride and hi-hat carry the groove and ensure fluency, whereas the snare and bass drum fill the gaps with jazz phrasing. Play the ride cymbal with the tip of your drumstick for maximum projection and aim for perfect unison and utilisation of your arm, wrist and fingers. This advanced hands technique is used most commonly by jazz drummers and is referred to as the Moeller method (Fig. 1).

Measure 1 | *Moeller method*

This is a combination of traditional jazz drumming techniques that have been developed over the years. The goal is to improve speed, power and control with the flexibility to add accented notes at will. If done well, it can be used in any style of drumming and will significantly enhance your technical ability. Books and DVDs by the late Jim Chapin will show you the rudiments and explain how to develop these with time. More modern applications of these techniques can be seen on videos by Steve Smith, Dave Weckl and Jojo Mayer.

B Section (Measures 13–24)

The B section is similar to the A section albeit with some variations. In measures 21 and 22 you have the opportunity to solo around the notated stabs, something which is common in jazz and, particularly, big band drumming.

C Section (Measures 25–33)

This is the second part of the lead melody where the groove is based on straight eighth instead of swung eight notes. This groove intensifies with rim-shot backbeat, heavier bass drum and hi-hat foot on every quarter note. Smoothly changing from swung to straight feel and vice versa is an important tool in drumming, regardless of your stylistic preference. The rhythmic indication above measure 32 indicates that the eighths should be swung again from this measure.

D Section (Measures 25–32)

The D section is essentially a 24 measure guitar solo that consists of two main grooves: one swung (from measure 34) and one straight (from measure 46).

E Section (Measures 58–65)

This is the drum solo, where you can demonstrate your musicality and stylistic understanding. The time signature changes to 6/4, so ensure that the pulse remains solid.

F Section (Measures 66–85)

The first seven measures feature a 6/4 groove with backbeat and fills. From measure 73 the time signature returns to the original 5/4 and the syncopated crash in measure 74 leads back to the beginning of the piece. Remember that when repeating the first eight measures of the A section the part should not be played as before but should instead be developed stylistically. The ***Coda*** section involves dynamic changes, stick on stick technique and changes from swung to straight feel.

Measure 79 | *Stick on stick*

Stick on stick is a jazz technique where one drumstick is hit by the other. This is most commonly done on the snare and can be used for various applications. In order to execute this well, place the tip of the stick held in your left hand on the snare and apply some pressure to the drum head (ensuring that the stick will not move while being struck). Next, use the neck part of the stick in your right hand and hit the other stick with the desired rhythm. Practise this technique and seek the best possible sound, or sweet spot (Fig. 2).

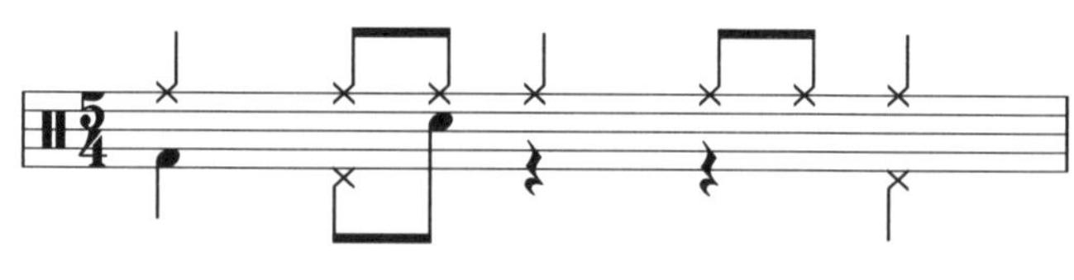

Fig. 1: Balance and sound in jazz

Fig. 2: Stick on stick

Technical Exercises

In this section the assessor will ask you to play a selection of exercises drawn from each of the five groups shown below. In Group F you will be asked to prepare ***one*** stylistic study from the three printed. The choice of stylistic study will determine the style of the Quick Study Piece. You do not need to memorise the exercises (and can use the book in the assessment) but the assessor will be looking for the speed of your response.

The stickings shown (L & R) are there as a guide for right handed drummers. Left handed drummers should reverse the sticking patterns. **All exercises must be played to a metronome click.** Groups A–D should be played at the tempo shown for each exercise.

Group A: Single Strokes

Single strokes in quarter notes, eighth notes, eighth-note triplets, 16th notes, quintuplet 16th notes, sextuplet 16th notes, septuplet 16th notes and 32nd notes. The tempo is ♩=65.

Group B: Paradiddles

Flam paradiddle in 16th notes and paradiddle-diddle in sextuplets with accents on toms. The tempo is ♩= 80.

Group C: Flams

Pataflafla. The tempo is ♩= 80.

Group D: Ratamacues

Double and single ratamacue phrase. The tempo is ♩= 80.

Group E: Rolls

1. Seven stroke roll phrase. The tempo is ♩= 85.

2. Nine stroke roll phrase with accents on toms. The tempo is ♩= 85.

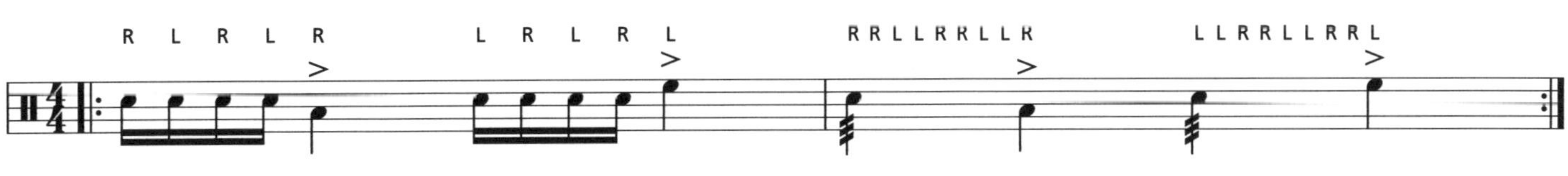

Group F: Stylistic Studies

You will prepare a technical study from one group of styles from the list below. Your choice of style will determine the style of the Quick Study Piece.

1. Rock/Metal: bell of ride 7/8 pattern, five stroke roll

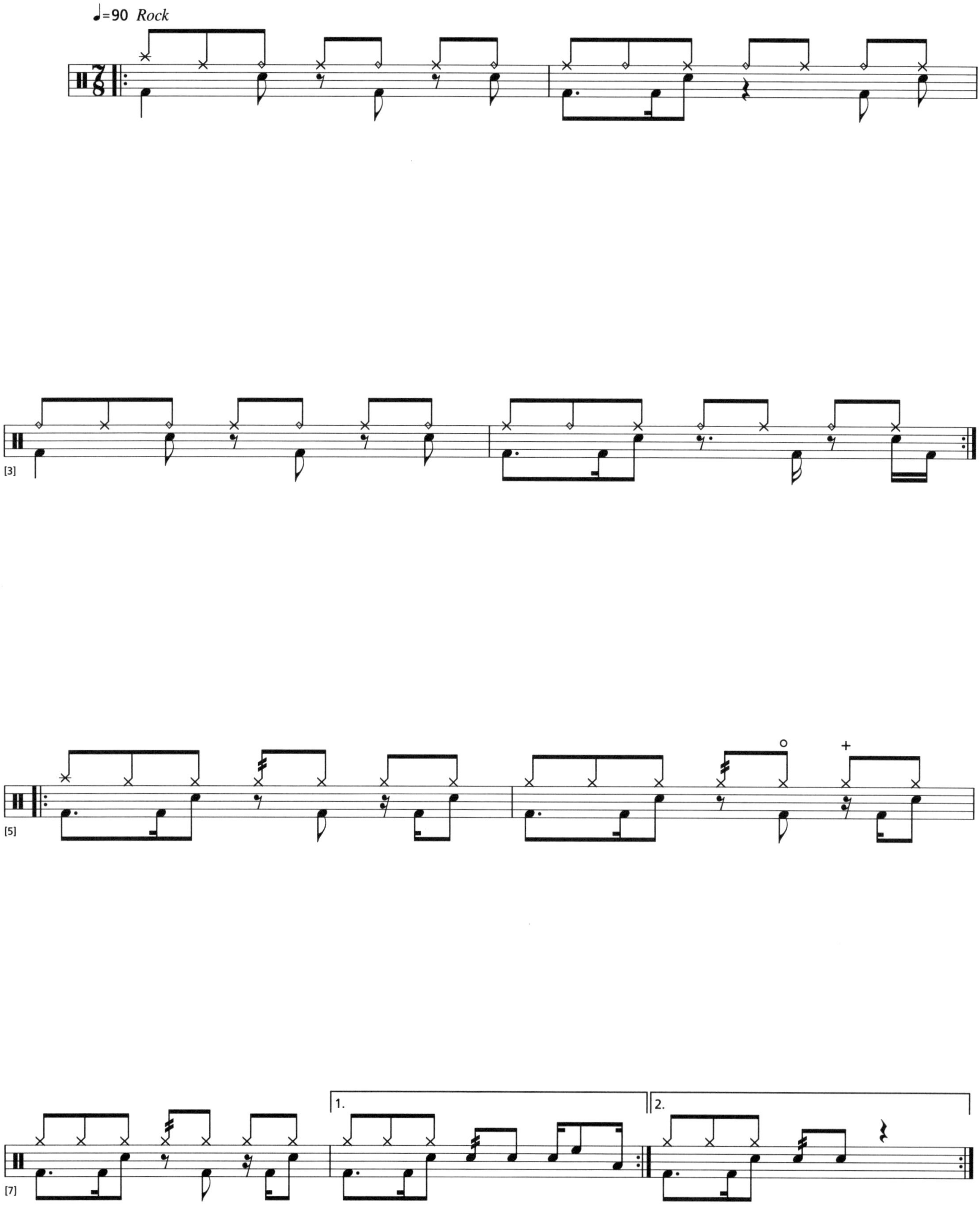

2. Funk: linear funk, nine stroke roll

3. Jazz/Latin/Blues: bell of ride 6/8 pattern, splashed hi-hats

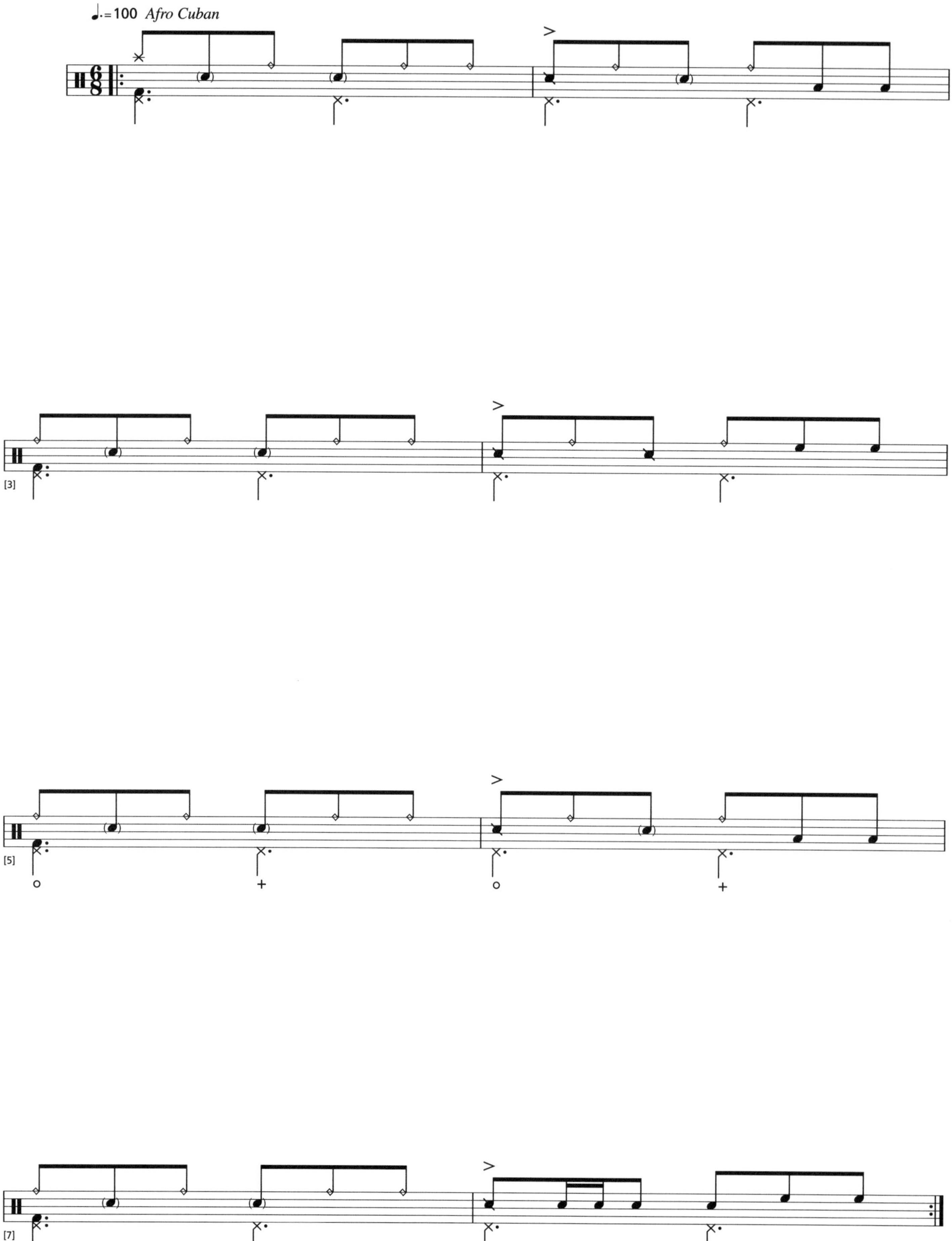

Quick Study Piece

At this level/grade you will be asked to prepare and play a short Quick Study Piece (QSP). Printed below are three examples of the type of QSP you are likely to receive in the assessment. You will be shown the test and played the track with the ***notated parts played***. Any measures that require improvisation will not be demonstrated. You will then have three minutes to study the test. The backing track will be played twice more. You will be allowed to practise during the first playing of the backing track, with the notated parts now absent, before playing it to the assessor on the second playing of the backing track.

The style of your QSP is determined by the stylistic study you selected in the technical exercise section. The QSP is in the form of a lead sheet and it is up to you to create your own interpretation of the music in the parts marked for improvisation.

Quick Study Piece

♩=110 Latin
[3]
Develop
[5]
[7]
[9]
[11]

Ear Tests

There are two Ear Tests in this level/grade. The assessor will play each test to you twice. You will find one example of each type of test printed below.

Test 1: Fill Playback and Recognition
The assessor will play you a one-measure fill in common time played on the snare drum. You will play back the fill on the snare drum. You will then identify the fill from three printed examples shown to you by the assessor. You will hear the test twice.

Each time the test is played it is preceded by a one-measure count in. There will be a short gap for you to practise. Next you will hear the vocal count in and you will then play the fill to the click. The tempo is ♩=70.

A

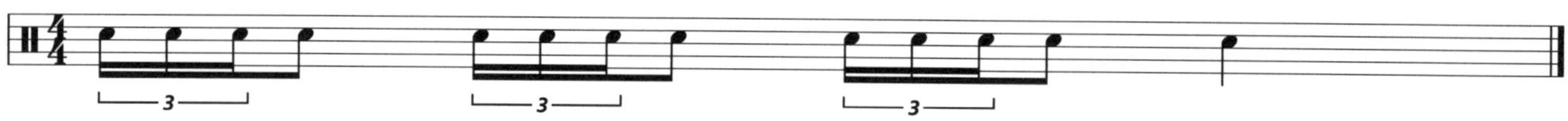

B

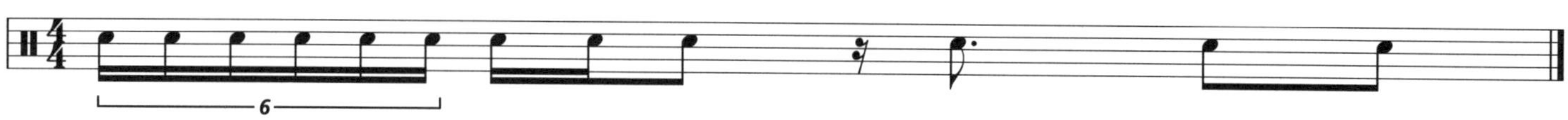

C

Test 2: Groove Recall
The assessor will play you a two-measure groove played on the whole kit. This is a two-measure groove repeated. You will hear the test twice. You will be asked to play the groove back on the drum voices indicated for four measures then identify the style from four choices given to you by the assessor.

Each time the test is played it is preceded by a one-measure vocal count-in. The tempo is ♩=80–140.

A: Blues
B: Trip Hop
C: Metal
D: Samba

♩=100

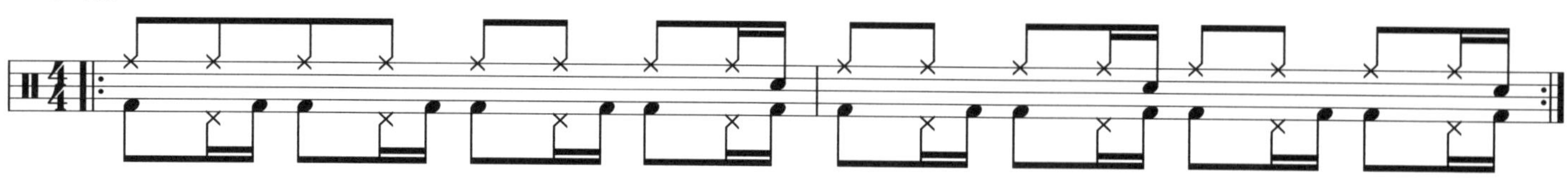

General Musicianship Questions

In this part of the assessment you will be asked five questions. Four of these questions will be about general music knowledge and the fifth question asked will be about your instrument.

Music Knowledge
The assessor will ask you four music knowledge questions based on a piece of music that you have played in the assessment. You will nominate the piece of music about which the questions will be asked. In this level/grade you will be asked to identify and demonstrate your answers on your instrument as directed by the assessor.

In Level/Grade 7 you will be asked to explain:

- Any notation used in the chosen piece
- Any dynamic marking found in the piece
- What makes the drum groove stylistically appropriate
- Use of drum voices, rhythms and techniques in drum solo sections

Instrument Knowledge
The assessor will also ask you one question regarding your instrument.

In Level/Grade 7 you will be asked to explain and demonstrate:

- Care and maintenance of drums and cymbals
- How to tune the drum kit according to the style of one of the pieces played
- How to produce: cross stick, choke cymbal, bell of ride, rim-shots, ghost notes, half open hi-hat, accents

Further Information
Tips on how to approach this part of this assessment can be found in the *Syllabus Guide* for Drums, the Rockschool *Drums Companion Guide* and on the Rockschool website: *www.rslawards.com.*

Entering Rockschool Assessments

Entering a Rockschool assessment is easy, just go online and follow our simple six step process. All details for entering online, dates, fees, regulations and Free Choice pieces can be found at *www.rslawards.com*

- All candidates should ensure they bring their own Level/Grade syllabus book to the assessment or have proof of digital purchase ready to show the assessor.

- All Level/Grade 6–8 candidates must ensure that they bring valid photo ID to their assessment.

Marking Schemes

Debut to Level/Grade 5 *

ELEMENT	PASS	MERIT	DISTINCTION
Performance Piece 1	12–14 out of 20	15–17 out of 20	18+ out of 20
Performance Piece 2	12–14 out of 20	15–17 out of 20	18+ out of 20
Performance Piece 3	12–14 out of 20	15–17 out of 20	18+ out of 20
Technical Exercises	9–10 out of 15	11–12 out of 15	13+ out of 15
Sight Reading *or* Improvisation & Interpretation	6 out of 10	7–8 out of 10	9+ out of 10
Ear Tests	6 out of 10	7–8 out of 10	9+ out of 10
General Musicianship Questions	3 out of 5	4 out of 5	5 out of 5
TOTAL MARKS	**60%+**	**74%+**	**90%+**

Levels/Grades 6–8

ELEMENT	PASS	MERIT	DISTINCTION
Performance Piece 1	12–14 out of 20	15–17 out of 20	18+ out of 20
Performance Piece 2	12–14 out of 20	15–17 out of 20	18+ out of 20
Performance Piece 3	12–14 out of 20	15–17 out of 20	18+ out of 20
Technical Exercises	9–10 out of 15	11–12 out of 15	13+ out of 15
Quick Study Piece	6 out of 10	7–8 out of 10	9+ out of 10
Ear Tests	6 out of 10	7–8 out of 10	9+ out of 10
General Musicianship Questions	3 out of 5	4 out of 5	5 out of 5
TOTAL MARKS	**60%+**	**74%+**	**90%+**

Performance Certificates | Debut to Level/Grade 8 *

ELEMENT	PASS	MERIT	DISTINCTION
Performance Piece 1	12–14 out of 20	15–17 out of 20	18+ out of 20
Performance Piece 2	12–14 out of 20	15–17 out of 20	18+ out of 20
Performance Piece 3	12–14 out of 20	15–17 out of 20	18+ out of 20
Performance Piece 4	12–14 out of 20	15–17 out of 20	18+ out of 20
Performance Piece 5	12–14 out of 20	15–17 out of 20	18+ out of 20
TOTAL MARKS	**60%+**	**75%+**	**90%+**

* Note that there are no Debut Vocal assessments.

Drums Notation Explained

BASS DRUM & TOMS

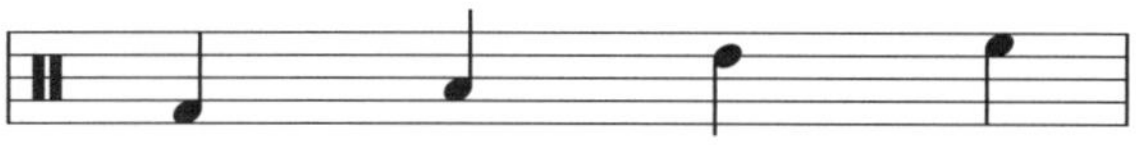

Bass drum | Floor tom | Medium tom | High tom

SNARE

Snare | Ghost snare | Rim-shot | Cross stick | Buzz snare

Rim-shot: *Strike snare drum and surrounding rim at same time*

Cross stick: *Place palm on snare drum head and strike rim with stick*

HI-HAT

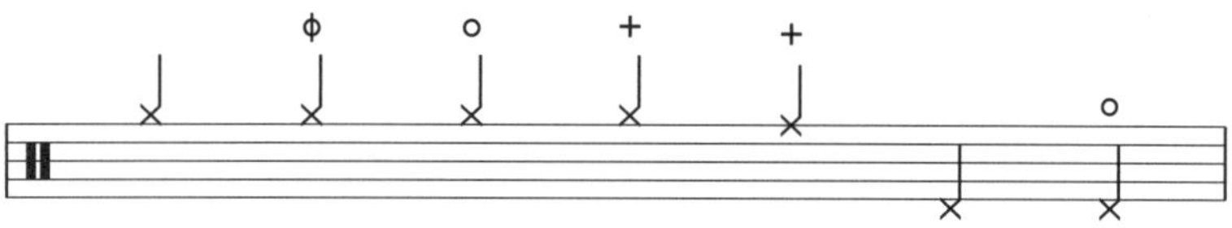

Closed | Half open | Open | Closed† | Closed‡ | Hi-hat foot closed | Hi-hat foot open

† Used on the first closed hi-hat that follows an open hi-hat

‡ The hi-hat is closed without being struck. Note that the hi-hat closed (cross) symbol may appear above drum voices other than the hi-hat (as shown above). This simply means another drum voice is being played at the same moment that the hi-hat is being closed.

OTHER CYMBALS

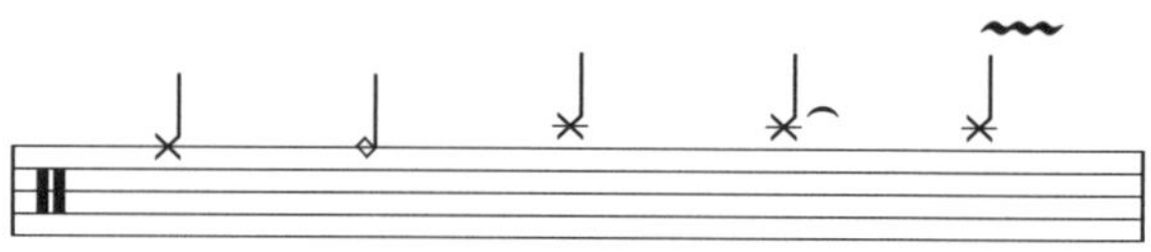

Ride | Ride (bell) | Crash | Crash* | Crash roll

***Allow all cymbals to ring on** unless explicitly stopped, as indicated by the keyword **'Choke'**. Occasionally ties may be used (*) to emphasise that cymbals should be allowed to ring on. This can avoid confusion during syncopations and pushes.*

GENERAL MUSIC NOTATION

Accentuate note (play it louder).

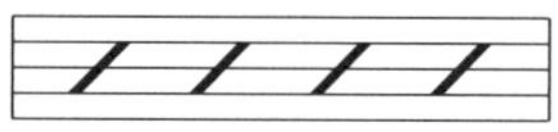

Slashes are used to demarcate measures during solos, fills, developments and other ad lib. sections.

D.𝄋. al Coda

Go back to the sign (𝄋) then play until the measure marked ***To Coda*** 𝄌 then skip to the section marked 𝄌 ***Coda***.

Repeat the measures between the repeat signs.

D.C. al Fine

Go back to beginning of song and play until the measure marked ***Fine*** (end).

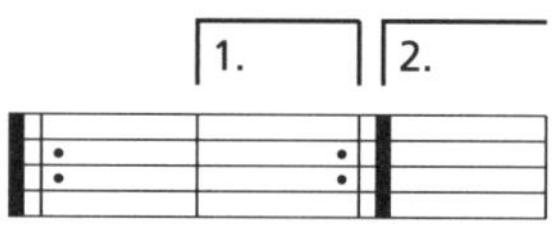

When a repeated section has different endings, play the first ending only the first time and the second ending only the second time.

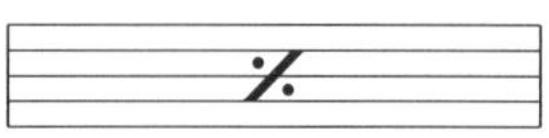

Repeat the previous measure. In higher levels/grades these may also be marked *sim.* or *cont. sim.*

Repeat the previous two measures. In higher levels/grades these may also be marked *sim.* or *cont. sim.*

In rudiments, each stem slash subdivides the note value by half.

MUSICAL TERMS WITH SPECIFIC EXAMINATION DEFINITIONS

Fill Play an individual, stylistic fill.

Cont. sim. Continue in similar way but vary the pattern slightly.

Develop Extend the musical part in a stylistically appropriate manner.

Rit. (ritardando) Gradually slow the tempo.

Mechanical Copyright Information

Family Affair
(Blige/Miller/Young/Bradford/Elizondo/Kambon/Louis/Lodge)
Warner/Chappell Music Limited/Kobalt Music Publishing Limited/Universal/MCA Music Limited/Spirit Music Publishing Limited/BMG Rights Management (UK) Limited

What Is Hip?
Words & Music by David Garibaldi, Stephen Kupka & Emilio Castillo
Sony/ATV Music Publishing (UK) Limited

Law
(Spaven/McCallum)
Richard Spaven/EMI Music Publishing Limited

Control
(Milton/Kennard/Goldman/Stanton/Dyas/Wink/Holman/Vincent)
Universal Music Publishing Limited/Bluewater Music UK/Downtown Music UK Limited

Cry Me A River
(Timberlake/Storch/Mosley)
Imagem Music/Warner/Chappell North America Limited/Reservoir Media Music

Techno
(Scofield)
Universal Music Publishing MGB Limited

mcps